PROPHETHOOD
AND THE PROPHET OF ISLAM

Ayatullah Ibrahim Amini

Translator:
Sayyid Athar Husain S. H. Rizvi

TABLE OF CONTENTS

Introduction *9*
Part One: Prophethood General Prophethood *12*
   Need for Prophethood 12

   Compilation of the program of success 17

Infallibility of the prophets *21*
   Philosophy of infallibility 23

Knowledge of the prophets *27*
   Prophets and the knowledge of Unseen 29

   Is the knowledge of Unseen only for Almighty Allah? 31

Miracle – a Testimony of Prophethood *35*
   Definition of Miracle 37

   Whose act is a Miracle? 38

   Difference between Miracle and Magic 40

Methods to recognize the prophet *43*
Revelation *46*
Number of Prophets *51*
Aims of the Prophets *53*
   The final aim of the prophets 57

Two world views *63*
   Materialistic world view 63

   Religious world view 64

   World view of the prophets 64

Foundation of the call of the prophets 66

Prophets and unity of method and aim 69

Perseverance of the Prophets... 76

Perseverance of Prophet Ibrahim.................................... 76

Perseverance of Prophet Musa 77

Perseverance of Prophet Muhammad 79

Part Two: Prophet of Islam Special Prophethood.............. 83

Evidences of the prophethood of Muhammad................ 83

Prophet of Islam and glad tidings about him 91

Prophet of Islam and Miracle 98

Quran – an everlasting Miracle.. 104

Aspects of the miracle of Quran 110

A New Style 110

Decisiveness in discourse 113

No contradiction between the verses 115

Information of the Unseen 118

Muhammad, the last prophet 126

Permanence of the laws of Islam.................................... 132

Why the sending of legislative prophets ended? 137

The Prophet before prophethood 142

Religion of Muhammad before 146

Ministry of Prophet Muhammad.. 153

Revelation and preservation of Quran 160

Paper of that time 164

Compilation of Quran 166

During the lifetime of the Holy Prophet 166

During Abu Bakr's tenure... 168

Compilation of Quran by Ali Ibn Abi Talib................... 171

During the Tenure of Uthman 173
Manner and morals of the Holy Prophet 177
Behavior with others 179
Behavior of the Prophet with his family members 182
Simplicity 183
Worship 184
Morals and manners of the Prophet in Quran 187
Some Qualities of the Prophet 190
Forgiveness despite having the power of revenge 192
Moderation and pardon 194
Generosity and forgiveness 196
Modesty 199
Prophet's activities inside the house 200
Prophet's activities outside the house 201
Behavior of the Prophet in gatherings 202
Behavior of the Prophet towards people in a gathering .. 203
Behavior of the Prophet with the youth 204
Bibliography 207

INTRODUCTION
In the name of Allah, the Beneficent, the Merciful

This world has not come into being on its own; on the contrary, it has a wise and an intelligent creator, who has created the universe with knowledge, power, intention and from the aspect of wisdom and He never does anything that is aimless and vain.

Creation of man and the world also is not vain and aimless. Man has not come into this world to live for a brief period of time, so that he may eat, drink, fulfill his sensual desires and then die and get annihilated. On the contrary, the wise Almighty Allah had a lofty aim in the creation of man. Man is created so that he may nurture his soul with faith, good deeds and fine morals and to prepare for the beautiful and everlasting life of the hereafter. Therefore man is not annihilated with death. Instead, he is transferred from this world to the abode of the hereafter. In that world, he sees the total consequences of his deed; the good and the righteous persons would get good rewards for their deeds and along with perfect and illuminated selves live in the everlasting Paradise forever and enjoy the different bounties of their merciful Lord and the oppressive and evil persons would also receive complete punishment commensurate to their misdeeds.

Therefore, this world is the harvest field of the hereafter and a place for building the self and developing spirituality; therefore one must prepare the provisions for the hereafter in this world itself. At this point, the following questions arise:

1. Is man needful of a perfect program and agenda in order to scale the stages of spiritual perfection and everlasting success and happiness?

2. Is it possible for man to prepare this agenda on his own? Or he is in need of the guidance of the creator of the world?

The reply to the first question is clear and it does not require any explanation, because man lives in a society and he cannot life a life of peace and comfort without the existence of a perfect and comprehensive law. Therefore there a law is necessary to guarantee the rights of others, prevention of oppressions and to maintain peace and order. Ideal and spiritual life of man is also in need of a plan and agenda. A program and agenda is also a must for the development and training of self and to guarantee success in the hereafter. Therefore, there is no doubt that man is in need of a perfect and a comprehensive agenda of action in order to secure his success in world and hereafter.

As for the reply to the second question, it calls for additional explanation and therefore the discussion of prophethood is unavoidable and it is first of all necessary to discuss it in detail and only then can we move forward. We shall discuss the topic of prophethood from two aspects: General points related to the origin of prophethood which is also called as 'General

Prophethood' and the second aspect is that of messengership and points related especially to Messenger of Islam, which is also termed as 'Special Prophethood'.

This book will discuss the above topics in two different parts; one part being exclusively with general prophethood and another related to the prophethood of The Holy Prophet Muhammad (ṣ) and the description of his proclamation as well as a sketch of his character and life history. It is hoped that the study of this book would step towards understanding the character of the prophets; especially that of Prophet Muhammad (ṣ).

Summer 1383

Qom, Ibrahim Amīnī

PART ONE:
PROPHETHOOD; GENERAL PROPHETHOOD

NEED FOR PROPHETHOOD

Almighty Allah has created man in the best of the forms and bestowed perfections for him and He has placed in his being, inclination to perfection and power of movement towards it. Man, in the course of his life and to guarantee the real success is in need of a program and guide and without them he cannot reach his aimed perfection. Man alone cannot recognize the program of life and the path of success and he does not know how to apply them. On the contrary, he is needful of the creator of the world and His prophets. Thus we conclude that it is necessary for the Almighty God to send prophets to guide mankind.

We shall study this subject under two topics:

First topic: Study of the need of man for a program of life and the special qualities of a successful program:

Second topic: Recognition of the compiler of the perfect program.

We shall explain the first topic under a few headings:

1. In logical sciences, it is proved that man is a compound of a body and a soul, from the aspect of the body, he is like other material things and is subject to change and movement; and from the aspect of the soul he is considered as a part of the abstract world. But in this very condition, each of them is related to another. Since the soul of man is related to a material body, and is not solely an abstract thing; it is having possibility of movement and desire for perfection. In the beginning, he is a weak being, which progresses gradually and becomes more and more perfect; but in all the stages there is only one reality and not more.

2. On one side, man is placed on path of perfection and by nature he is desirous of perfection and on the other hand, he is equipped with the power of acquiring perfection, therefore it is possible for him to reach perfection; hence there is no vain act in the system of God's creation. Since every material being can reach its possible perfection, man is also not deprived of this great divine bounty and he can reach his desired perfection; on the contrary Almighty Allah has prepared for him the way to achieve this.

3. Man is having two kinds of lives: one of them is the life of the world, which is related to his body; and the other is the spiritual and inward life, related to his soul. As a result of this in accordance with each of these two lives, he will either have perfection and success or decline and misfortune.

Man is busy in the life of the world and it is possible that he might be become unmindful of his spiritual life, but he is also having a real life in his inner being, which in the end will either take him to salvation and perfection of humanity or lead him to an everlasting decline and evil resort.

Therefore, correct beliefs, good manners and good deeds, are means for perfection of soul and inner success, because false beliefs, bad habits and improper behaviors make a man deviate from the straight path and take him to the valley of destruction and evil.

If man is on the straight path of perfection, the essence of his being gains maturity and after traversing stages of perfection to his real condition, which is the condition of luminosity and happiness, he scales them. But if he sacrifices the spiritual perfections, good ethics and excellent character on the altar of sensual and animal desires or in shape of beastly infatuations, he would become deviated from the straight path of humanity and fall into the ravine of destruction and evil.

4. Just as there is perfect unity and attachment between the body and soul of man, there is also a relationship between the life of the world and spiritual life. And it is not possible to separate the two of them and make each of them independent entities.

Good or bad deeds and character of man, without any doubt will have good or bad effect on his self; since the qualities and capacities have effect on the howness of incidence of acts. The spiritual and inner life of man is the source of his beliefs, character and acts. Without correct faith and performance of good deeds, he cannot reach his intended stage of perfection and spiritual success, just as without purification of self it is not possible to reform ones acts and to gain perfect good sense.

5. Man lives in the society and derives all kinds of benefits from it and also passes on benefits to them. But there are instances when a person may not pass on the benefit or may trespass on the rights of others; and this would make life in society very difficult. That is why human society is needful of a perfect, precise and comprehensive sat of laws so that it can guarantee the rights of people and prevent the trespassing on the rights of others.

Therefore, since man is having two dimensions of existence (body and soul) and two kinds of life, which have perfect relationship with each other, he is in need of a program and course of action to gain success in both his lives; which has the success of the world as well as everlasting success in the hereafter; in such a way that it neither sacrifices the life of the hereafter on the life of the world and neither does it gives up the spiritual life for the comfort of the life of this world. It is such a program, which is compiled according to the actual needs of man and which leads man on the path of success and salvation and not on an imaginative and hypothetical perfection. A program, which is based on human excellence and perfection and which calls the attention of man for growth of his ethereal soul and inclines him to the position of divine proximity and thus he begins to consider the world as the harvest field of the hereafter. In compilation and arrangement of these laws, real benefits of all human beings are kept in view and narrow mindedness, improper prejudice and groupism are avoided. Almighty Allah says:

يَٰٓأَيُّهَا ٱلَّذِينَ ءَامَنُواْ ٱسْتَجِيبُواْ لِلَّهِ وَلِلرَّسُولِ إِذَا دَعَاكُمْ لِمَا يُحْيِيكُمْ وَٱعْلَمُوٓاْ أَنَّ

$$\text{اللَّهَ يَحُولُ بَيْنَ الْمَرْءِ وَقَلْبِهِ وَأَنَّهُ إِلَيْهِ تُحْشَرُونَ ﴿٢٤﴾}$$

"O you who believe! answer (the call of) Allah and His Apostle when he calls you to that which gives you life; and know that Allah intervenes between man and his heart, and that to Him you shall be gathered." (8:24)

$$\text{يَا أَيُّهَا النَّاسُ قَدْ جَاءَكُم بُرْهَانٌ مِّن رَّبِّكُمْ وَأَنزَلْنَا إِلَيْكُمْ نُورًا مُّبِينًا ﴿١٧٤﴾ فَأَمَّا الَّذِينَ ءَامَنُوا بِاللَّهِ وَاعْتَصَمُوا بِهِ فَسَيُدْخِلُهُمْ فِي رَحْمَةٍ مِّنْهُ وَفَضْلٍ وَيَهْدِيهِمْ إِلَيْهِ صِرَاطًا مُّسْتَقِيمًا ﴿١٧٥﴾}$$

"O people! surely there has come to you manifest proof from your Lord and We have sent to you clear light. Then as for those who believe in Allah and hold fast by Him, He will cause them to enter into His mercy and grace and guide them to Himself on a right path." (173-174)

$$\text{كَانَ النَّاسُ أُمَّةً وَاحِدَةً فَبَعَثَ اللَّهُ النَّبِيِّينَ مُبَشِّرِينَ وَمُنذِرِينَ وَأَنزَلَ مَعَهُمُ الْكِتَابَ بِالْحَقِّ لِيَحْكُمَ بَيْنَ النَّاسِ فِيمَا اخْتَلَفُوا فِيهِ وَمَا اخْتَلَفَ فِيهِ إِلَّا الَّذِينَ أُوتُوهُ مِن بَعْدِ مَا جَاءَتْهُمُ الْبَيِّنَاتُ بَغْيًا بَيْنَهُمْ فَهَدَى اللَّهُ الَّذِينَ ءَامَنُوا لِمَا اخْتَلَفُوا فِيهِ مِنَ الْحَقِّ بِإِذْنِهِ وَاللَّهُ يَهْدِي مَن يَشَاءُ إِلَىٰ صِرَاطٍ مُّسْتَقِيمٍ ﴿٢١٣﴾}$$

"(All) people are a single nation; so Allah raised prophets as bearers of good news and as warners, and He revealed with them the Book with truth, that it might judge between people in that in which they differed; and none but the very people who were given it differed about it after clear arguments had come to them, revolting among themselves; so Allah has guided by His will those who believe to the truth about which they differed and Allah guides whom He pleases to the right path." (2:213)

Compilation of the program of success

After we have become aware of conditions and specialties of a perfect program, the question arises that who is supposed to design and compile this program? Whether all human beings or intellectuals, intelligent beings or reformers are capable of designing such a program?

With a little thought we can conclude that the reply to this is a decisive 'no', because:

Firstly: One who can occupy this post of designing such a program should have real cognition of man and he should be aware of the secrets and subtleties of the body and ethereal soul of man and he should also have knowledge about the aims and inclinations and the positive and negative points of man and the demands of time and space and occurrence of hardships as also their laws and effects; while the fact is that such a person cannot be found among human beings.

Secondly: Even if we suppose that human law makers can design such a program for administration of worldly matters of human beings, without any doubt, they do not have sufficient awareness about the secrets and mysteries of the ethereal soul of man, and the ideal needs and spiritual life, from the deep relationship between the life of the world and the inner life and also from the perfection of soul and causes of the decline of man. That is why man himself cannot to design for himself a perfect and complete program of life, and basically control the spiritual life of man with attention to the development of ethereal soul of human beings, which is beyond the scope of lawmakers of humanity.

That is why man is not capable to frame laws to guarantee peace and prosperity of his worldly life and to design a program to assure success of his life in hereafter. Thus the only one who can design a perfect and compatible program and entrust it to man, is God, creator of the world and man, who is perfectly aware of make up and being of man, secrets and subtleties and who is well aware of all his needs, aspirations and inclinations. It is Him alone who is aware of the real perfections of man and well knows the causes of the exaltation and decline of the soul. It is only the wise God, who sees the world of human beings equally, and all the human beings are His creatures. He loves all and is desirous of their success and salvation. He is never selfish, narrow minded and prejudiced.

Yes, it is only God who can lay down the program to guarantee success of the body and soul and world and the hereafter of man and entrust it to His chosen prophets. It is Him that His unlimited grace has caused the performance of this action and has not deprived the people from this great divine bounty. It is God, who has provided causes for the perfection for different types of material beings so that they may be able to through their actions and efforts to reach their intended aim. The Holy Quran says:

$$رَبُّنَا الَّذِي أَعْطَىٰ كُلَّ شَيْءٍ خَلْقَهُ ثُمَّ هَدَىٰ$$

"Our Lord is He Who gave to everything its creation, then guided it (to its goal)." (20:50)

A God, who created man with this greatness and in creation of his body and soul placed thousands of secrets and mysteries and appointed the material world at his disposal; it is not possible that He should become oblivious of his success, real perfection and actual aim of his existence and that he should not give him the capability reach this aim.

Through this is proved the need of prophets and their message. Almighty Allah, in order to convey His message to man, selected some persons from among them, so that He may through them send His programs and laws with regard to their needs. Thus prophets are selected human beings who convey the message of God and guide to success and perfection and warn of the factors of decline and misfortune. Almighty Allah says:

$$\text{بَنِى ءَادَمَ إِمَّا يَأْتِيَنَّكُمْ رُسُلٌ مِنكُمْ يَقُصُّونَ عَلَيْكُمْ ءَايَتِي فَمَنِ ٱتَّقَىٰ وَأَصْلَحَ فَلَا خَوْفٌ عَلَيْهِمْ وَلَا هُمْ يَحْزَنُونَ ۝ وَٱلَّذِينَ كَذَّبُوا۟ بِـَٔايَتِنَا وَٱسْتَكْبَرُوا۟ عَنْهَآ أُو۟لَٰٓئِكَ أَصْحَٰبُ ٱلنَّارِ هُمْ فِيهَا خَٰلِدُونَ ۝}$$

"O children of Adam! if there come to you apostles from among you relating to you My communications, then whoever shall guard (against evil) and act aright- they shall have no fear nor shall they grieve. And (as for) those who reject Our communications and turn away from them haughtily- these are the inmates of the fire, they shall abide in it." (7:35-36)

$$\text{وَمَا نُرْسِلُ ٱلْمُرْسَلِينَ إِلَّا مُبَشِّرِينَ وَمُنذِرِينَ فَمَنْ ءَامَنَ وَأَصْلَحَ فَلَا خَوْفٌ عَلَيْهِمْ وَلَا هُمْ يَحْزَنُونَ ۝ وَٱلَّذِينَ كَذَّبُوا۟ بِـَٔايَتِنَا يَمَسُّهُمُ ٱلْعَذَابُ بِمَا كَانُوا۟ يَفْسُقُونَ ۝}$$

"And We send not messengers but as announcers of good news and givers of warning, then whoever believes and acts aright, they shall have no fear, nor shall they grieve. And (as for) those who reject Our communications, chastisement shall afflict them because they transgressed." (6:48-49)

وَلَقَدْ بَعَثْنَا فِى كُلِّ أُمَّةٍ رَسُولًا أَنِ اعْبُدُوا اللَّهَ وَاجْتَنِبُوا الطَّاغُوتَ ۖ فَمِنْهُم مَّنْ هَدَى اللَّهُ وَمِنْهُم مَّنْ حَقَّتْ عَلَيْهِ الضَّلَالَةُ ۚ فَسِيرُوا فِى الْأَرْضِ فَانظُرُوا كَيْفَ كَانَ عَاقِبَةُ الْمُكَذِّبِينَ ۝

"And certainly We raised in every nation an apostle saying: Serve Allah and shun the Shaitan. So there were some of them whom Allah guided and there were others against whom error was due; therefore travel in the land, then see what was the end of the rejecters." (16:36)

INFALLIBILITY OF THE PROPHETS

Almighty Allah selected the prophets so that they may entrust the human beings with laws and life-giving program of religion in a perfect way without adding or subtracting anything. That they may show man the straight path of perfection and divine proximity and it is one path and not more. And also that they may help human beings on the path of salvation and perfection; that they take up the responsibility of guardianship and leadership of nation and implementation of divine laws and development of excellence of man.

Responsibility of the prophets in this regard is explained in three stages:

1. They receive laws and programs of religion through the channel of revelation;

2. They convey the divine programs and messages to human beings;

3. They themselves act on the rules and regulations of religion and also call people to divine religion through their words and deeds.

The aim of Almighty Allah in sending mortal prophets assures that they should be infallible in these three stages; that is they should be immune from mistakes, doubts and forgetfulness in receiving the divine messages and conveying them to the people. In case they are not infallible, how can they convey the life-giving program of religion without any alteration and without any increase or decrease to people? In that case would the aim of the wise God in sending the prophets be achieved perfectly? Can people gain satisfaction and assurance that the statements of the prophets are the same message of God and program of religion? No, it is never in this way, on the contrary divine prophets should be immune from errors, doubts and forgetfulness so that they may be able to convey the programs of religion without any increase or decrease and that they may guarantee the fulfillment of the aim of Almighty Allah.

Prophets in the stage of acting on the laws of religion also must be infallible; that is they should fulfill the duties and obligatory acts and keep away from prohibited matters, sins and evil deeds. Because they are perfect examples of religion and by their actions they call people to good deeds and restrain them from evil deeds. If the prophets are not infallible, how can they take up the responsibility of guiding the humanity and how they can invite people to good deeds?

People do not trust one who is himself deviated and who is having contradiction between his words and deeds; since they say: If he was truthful and had believed in his own words, he would have acted according to them. In that case most probably they would prefer to follow their acts and not their words (supposing they were not in consonance with their prophethood). Therefore Almighty Allah will never send such a person as a prophet.

Hence the intellect of man testifies to the necessity of infallibility of prophets and there is no need to quote more verses of Quran or traditions to emphasize this matter. But in the coming pages we would quote some of them by way of textual proofs.

Philosophy of infallibility

In the past discussion we concluded that prophets are immune from sins, mistakes and forgetfulness. Now the question arises that what is the philosophy of infallibility? Why some people are infallible and why some are not? Since all human beings are prone to commit mistakes, how can some persons be immune from errors? What factor bestows to human beings such a power and immunity that they can dominate their selfish desires and don't even think of committing sins? What is the real motive and aim of this immunity?

According to our belief, infallibility is a quality of the soul and a powerful inner capacity, which restrains the infallible from committing sin and falling into doubt and other similar things. The factor and aim of the existence of this quality is perfect faith, which is beyond the stage of meaning and mental imagination and which has come into the shape of a certainty and actual realization. People who have reached to the lofty stages of knowing Almighty Allah and have faith in resurrection and through the inner conscience have witnessed the greatness and majesty of the Lord of the universe; and who are aware of the effects of deeds, good manners as also the consequences of following bad ethics and character are aloof from sins and disobedience and with insight and from the aspect of choice and intention, they were obedient to divine laws and control their selfish desires and under no circumstances cross the divinely ordained limits of servitude and submission.

On the other hand, the existence of this insight is a strong support, which prevents them from committing mistakes and forgetfulness in receiving divine revelation and in conveying them to the people. They have realized the truth of divine messages and possess the treasures of unseen knowledge. It is due to this same reason that they are immune from mistakes and errors.

Since the existence of such a perfect and infallible man is necessary for prophethood, Allah, the Mighty and Sublime has arranged the system of creation in such a way that when needed, such a person would be available.

It is said that although the prophet is infallible and does not commit any kind of sin, it is not that the capacity of committing sins has been taken away from him. Instead, the prophet is also like other people; he is capable enough to commit sins and has the choice to commit them; at the most, under the influence of a strong faith and perfect insight, which is placed in his being as a divine gift, by choice and intention he gives up evil deeds and does not fall into divine disobedience.

Below we present some examples of strong evidences which prove that it is necessary for divine prophets to be infallible:

Almighty Allah says in the Holy Quran:

عَـٰلِمُ ٱلۡغَيۡبِ فَلَا يُظۡهِرُ عَلَىٰ غَيۡبِهِۦٓ أَحَدًا ۝ إِلَّا مَنِ ٱرۡتَضَىٰ مِن رَّسُولٍ فَإِنَّهُۥ يَسۡلُكُ مِنۢ بَيۡنِ يَدَيۡهِ وَمِنۡ خَلۡفِهِۦ رَصَدًا ۝ لِّيَعۡلَمَ أَن قَدۡ أَبۡلَغُواْ رِسَـٰلَـٰتِ رَبِّهِمۡ وَأَحَاطَ بِمَا لَدَيۡهِمۡ وَأَحۡصَىٰ كُلَّ شَيۡءٍ عَدَدَۢا ۝

"The Knower of the unseen! so He does not reveal His secrets to any. Except to him whom He chooses as an apostle; for surely He makes a guard to march before him and after him. So that He may know that they have truly delivered the messages of their Lord, and He encompasses what is with them, and He records the number of all things." (72:26-28)

Allamah Tabatabai has written under the exegesis of this verse:

Apparently this verse shows that Almighty Allah has chosen the prophets for divine revelation and also gave them a hidden power which accords protection to them. It is that Almighty Allah has surrounded the prophets in order to guard revelation from destruction and change which Satan or others may undertake. This is due to the joining of prophethood to the stage of manifestation. Similar to this verse is the verse in which it is mentioned in the words of angels:

(And we do not descend but by the command of your Lord; (Know that) to Him belongs whatever is before us and whatever is behind us and whatever is between these, and your Lord is not forgetful.)

The verses prove that divine revelation from the beginning of revelation till the time it reaches to the ears of man are in protection and are guarded from every kind of alteration.[1]

Also it has come in the same background that

أُوْلَٰٓئِكَ ٱلَّذِينَ هَدَى ٱللَّهُ فَبِهُدَىٰهُمُ ٱقْتَدِهْ:

---

[1] *Al-Mizan*, Vol. 2, Pg. 139

"These are they whom Allah guided, therefore follow their guidance." (6:90)

This proves the infallibility of the prophets; thus all of them are guided and Allah says:

$$\text{وَمَن يُضْلِلِ ٱللَّهُ فَمَا لَهُۥ مِنْ هَادٍ}$$

"...and (as for) him whom Allah makes err, there is no guide for him." (39:23)

$$\text{وَمَن يَهْدِ ٱللَّهُ فَمَا لَهُۥ مِن مُّضِلٍّ}$$

"And whom Allah guides, there is none that can lead him astray." (39:37)

And He also says:

$$\text{مَن يَهْدِ ٱللَّهُ فَهُوَ ٱلْمُهْتَدِى}$$

"Whomsoever Allah guides, he is the one who follows the right way." (7:178)

Thus Almighty Allah has kept immune His guided ones from every deviated and all kinds of deviations, which want to gain an upper hand on them. That is He has kept them safe from every kind of disobedience since disobedience is also a kind of misguidance.[1]

---

[1] *Al-Mizan*, Vol. 2, Pg. 140

KNOWLEDGE OF THE PROPHETS

Knowledge of the prophets through the channel of revelation originates from the limitless knowledge of God. Almighty Allah raised the prophets in order to convey the laws and programs of religion to human beings in a perfect way. They make efforts in guidance and hand over the causes of perfection and success to the people. That is why the prophets are supposed to be aware of all the matters connected with religion, which the people might be in need of so that they may be able to fulfill the aim of Almighty Allah in sending them to humanity.

Allah, the Mighty and Sublime has not left the success giving program of religion as defective and ambiguous and does not deprive people from the path of perfection and proximity. Therefore there is no other way to guide and instruct the people other than the channel of prophets, hence they should be perfectly cognizant of all the programs of religion.

Sciences necessary for prophethood can be divided into the following:

1. Perfect recognition of God, His names and qualities;

2. Perfect recognition of the world of Purgatory (*Barzakh*) and its specialties; complete awareness of the circumstances of Judgment Day, accounting, scroll of deeds, balance of deeds, Paradise and Hell.

3. Complete cognition of human soul and spiritual diseases and the methods of prevention and cures of these spiritual diseases; identification of good and bad morals and the method of purifying the soul and discipline and perfection of the self.

4. Complete knowledge of all the laws and programs of religion, following which can guarantee the success of man in the world and the hereafter.

The prophet should have complete knowledge of all the above mentioned points so that he may be able to guide the people on the straight path of religion. If he himself is not having knowledge, how he would be able to guide the people? Therefore, the God who sent prophets for the guidance of people, it is not possible that He should keep these prophets deprived of the necessary knowledge.

This point is mentioned in a number of verses of the Holy Quran. For example:

لَقَدۡ أَرۡسَلۡنَا رُسُلَنَا بِٱلۡبَيِّنَٰتِ وَأَنزَلۡنَا مَعَهُمُ ٱلۡكِتَٰبَ وَٱلۡمِيزَانَ لِيَقُومَ ٱلنَّاسُ بِٱلۡقِسۡطِ

"Certainly We sent Our apostles with clear arguments, and sent down with them the Book and the balance that men may conduct themselves with equity..." (57:25)

On another occasion He says:

وَوَهَبۡنَا لَهُۥٓ إِسۡحَٰقَ وَيَعۡقُوبَ كُلًّا هَدَيۡنَا وَنُوحًا هَدَيۡنَا مِن قَبۡلُ وَمِن ذُرِّيَّتِهِۦ دَاوُۥدَ وَسُلَيۡمَٰنَ وَأَيُّوبَ وَيُوسُفَ وَمُوسَىٰ وَهَٰرُونَ وَكَذَٰلِكَ نَجۡزِي ٱلۡمُحۡسِنِينَ ۝ وَزَكَرِيَّا وَيَحۡيَىٰ وَعِيسَىٰ وَإِلۡيَاسَ كُلٌّ مِّنَ ٱلصَّٰلِحِينَ ۝ وَإِسۡمَٰعِيلَ وَٱلۡيَسَعَ وَيُونُسَ وَلُوطًا وَكُلًّا فَضَّلۡنَا عَلَى ٱلۡعَٰلَمِينَ ۝ وَمِنۡ ءَابَآئِهِمۡ وَذُرِّيَّٰتِهِمۡ وَإِخۡوَٰنِهِمۡ وَٱجۡتَبَيۡنَٰهُمۡ

Knowledge of the Prophets

وَهَدَيْنَـٰهُمْ إِلَىٰ صِرَٰطٍ مُّسْتَقِيمٍ ۝ ذَٰلِكَ هُدَى ٱللَّهِ يَهْدِى بِهِۦ مَن يَشَآءُ مِنْ عِبَادِهِۦ ۚ وَلَوْ أَشْرَكُوا۟ لَحَبِطَ عَنْهُم مَّا كَانُوا۟ يَعْمَلُونَ ۝ أُو۟لَـٰٓئِكَ ٱلَّذِينَ ءَاتَيْنَـٰهُمُ ٱلْكِتَـٰبَ وَٱلْحُكْمَ وَٱلنُّبُوَّةَ ۚ فَإِن يَكْفُرْ بِهَا هَـٰٓؤُلَآءِ فَقَدْ وَكَّلْنَا بِهَا قَوْمًا لَّيْسُوا۟ بِهَا بِكَـٰفِرِينَ ۝ أُو۟لَـٰٓئِكَ ٱلَّذِينَ هَدَى ٱللَّهُ فَبِهُدَىٰهُمُ ٱقْتَدِهْ ۗ قُل لَّآ أَسْـَٔلُكُمْ عَلَيْهِ أَجْرًا ۖ إِنْ هُوَ إِلَّا ذِكْرَىٰ لِلْعَـٰلَمِينَ ۝

"And We gave to him Ishaq and Yaqub; each did We guide, and Nuh did We guide before, and of his descendants, Dawood and Sulaiman and Ayyub and Yusuf and Musa and Harun; and thus do We reward those who do good (to others). And Zakariya and Yahya and Isa and Ilyas; every one was of the good; and Ismail and Al-Yasha and Yunus and Lut; and every one We made to excel (in) the worlds: and from among their fathers and their descendants and their brethren, and We chose them and guided them into the right way. This is Allah's guidance, He guides thereby whom He pleases of His servants; and if they had set up others (with Him), certainly what they did would have become ineffectual for them. These are they to whom We gave the book and the wisdom and the prophecy; therefore if these disbelieve in it We have already entrusted with it a people who are not disbelievers in it. These are they whom Allah guided, therefore follow their guidance. Say: I do not ask you for any reward for it; it is nothing but a reminder to the nations." (6:84-90)

Prophets and the knowledge of Unseen

Existing things can generally be divided into two groups. Hidden (unseen) things, called as the world of *Ghaib* and world of seen beings, which is called as the world of visibility.

Beings and things which can be perceived through the five senses are included in the world of visibility; like matter, body and generally all its effects and specialties, like colors, quantities, forms, foods, smells, voices, softness and hardness, heat and cold and generally all matter and material things are included in this world of visibility. Things which man can perceive through his senses and about which he can gain knowledge.

World of the unseen is opposed to the world of visibility and all the beings that are beyond matter and materiality are included in the world of unseen. Like God, His names and qualities, angels, world of Purgatory (*Barzakh*), existing things of Barzakh, Judgment Day, Paradise and Hell, bounties of Paradise and chastisements of the hereafter; existences of these types are abstract things and they are superior to matter. Therefore they are included in the world of unseen. That is why we cannot maintain contact with the unseen world with our senses and create knowledge about it. This understanding and intelligence of ours for the unseen world should have been obtained through a channel other than the senses, which in terminology is called as knowledge of unseen.

Through the five senses we can only maintain contact with the things of the world of matter and we gain knowledge directly or indirectly, although in those instances also our knowledge is limited and conditional. Our eyes see, but only those that which possesses a particular volume and which is at a particular distance and having some special conditions of space and time. If that thing is very tiny or it is at a long distance of time or space from us or it is in darkness or there is something obstructing our view, it cannot be seen by us. Events of the period of Prophet Nuh (a) or a thousand years after that cannot be seen by us. We cannot with the help of the tools of our knowledge get connected to those events directly. They are unseen from us. Although they exist in the presence of God and He has knowledge of all of them; He encompasses all the existing things of the world of matter and the unseen. In the Holy Quran, He says:

$$\text{عَالِمُ ٱلْغَيْبِ وَٱلشَّهَادَةِ وَهُوَ ٱلْحَكِيمُ ٱلْخَبِيرُ}$$

"Knower of the unseen and the seen; and He is the Wise, the Aware." (6:73)

$$\text{وَلِلَّهِ غَيْبُ ٱلسَّمَٰوَٰتِ وَٱلْأَرْضِ}$$

"And Allah's is the unseen in the heavens and the earth..." (11:123)

$$\text{إِنَّ ٱللَّهَ يَعْلَمُ غَيْبَ ٱلسَّمَٰوَٰتِ وَٱلْأَرْضِ}$$

"Surely Allah knows the unseen things of the heavens and the earth." (49:18)

$$\text{ذَٰلِكَ مِنْ أَنۢبَآءِ ٱلْغَيْبِ نُوحِيهِ إِلَيْكَ}$$

"This is of the announcements relating to the unseen which We reveal to you..." (3:44)

Is the knowledge of Unseen only for Allah?

At this point, a question arises: Whether the knowledge of the unseen is restricted only to Almighty Allah; or human beings can also become aware of it? Some intellectuals consider the knowledge of unseen to be restricted only to Almighty Allah and they have reasoned through verses of Quran, like:

$$\text{وَعِندَهُ مَفَاتِحُ ٱلْغَيْبِ لَا يَعْلَمُهَا إِلَّا هُوَ}$$

"And with Him are the keys of the unseen treasures – none knows them but He..." (6:59)

$$\text{وَيَقُولُونَ لَوْلَا أُنزِلَ عَلَيْهِ ءَايَةٌ مِّن رَّبِّهِ ۖ فَقُلْ إِنَّمَا ٱلْغَيْبُ لِلَّهِ فَٱنتَظِرُوٓا إِنِّى مَعَكُم مِّنَ ٱلْمُنتَظِرِينَ}$$

"And they say: Why is not a sign sent to him from his Lord? Say: The unseen is only for Allah; therefore wait – surely I too, with you am of those who wait." (10:20)

$$\text{قُل لَّا يَعْلَمُ مَن فِى ٱلسَّمَٰوَٰتِ وَٱلْأَرْضِ ٱلْغَيْبَ إِلَّا ٱللَّهُ ۚ وَمَا يَشْعُرُونَ أَيَّانَ يُبْعَثُونَ}$$

"Say: No one in the heavens and the earth knows the unseen but Allah; and they do not know when they shall be raised." (27:65)

$$\text{قُل لَّآ أَقُولُ لَكُمْ عِندِى خَزَآئِنُ ٱللَّهِ وَلَآ أَعْلَمُ ٱلْغَيْبَ وَلَآ أَقُولُ لَكُمْ إِنِّى مَلَكٌ ۖ إِنْ أَتَّبِعُ إِلَّا مَا يُوحَىٰٓ إِلَىَّ ۚ قُلْ هَلْ يَسْتَوِى ٱلْأَعْمَىٰ وَٱلْبَصِيرُ ۗ أَفَلَا تَتَفَكَّرُونَ}$$

"Say: I do not say to you, I have with me the treasures of Allah, nor do I know the unseen, nor do I say to you that I am an angel; I do not follow aught save that which is revealed to me. Say: Are the blind and the seeing one alike? Do you not then reflect?" (6:50)

$$\text{قُل لَّآ أَمْلِكُ لِنَفْسِى نَفْعًا وَلَا ضَرًّا إِلَّا مَا شَآءَ ٱللَّهُ ۚ وَلَوْ كُنتُ أَعْلَمُ ٱلْغَيْبَ لَٱسْتَكْثَرْتُ مِنَ ٱلْخَيْرِ وَمَا مَسَّنِىَ ٱلسُّوٓءُ ۚ إِنْ أَنَا۠ إِلَّا نَذِيرٌ وَبَشِيرٌ لِّقَوْمٍ يُؤْمِنُونَ}$$

"Say: I do not control any benefit or harm for my own soul except as Allah please; and had I known the unseen I would have had much of good and no evil would have touched me; I am nothing but a warner and the giver of good news to a people who believe." (7:188)

They have reasoned through the apparent meaning of these verses and have said: Knowledge of unseen is only with Almighty Allah and human beings are ignorant of it.

But through other verses it can be concluded that there are some human beings also have access to this knowledge of unseen. For example:

عَٰلِمُ ٱلْغَيْبِ فَلَا يُظْهِرُ عَلَىٰ غَيْبِهِۦٓ أَحَدًا ۝ إِلَّا مَنِ ٱرْتَضَىٰ مِن رَّسُولٍ فَإِنَّهُۥ

يَسْلُكُ مِنۢ بَيْنِ يَدَيْهِ وَمِنْ خَلْفِهِۦ رَصَدًا ۝

"The Knower of the unseen! so He does not reveal His secrets to any. Except to him whom He chooses as an apostle; for surely He makes a guard to march before him and after him." (72:26-28)

مَّا كَانَ ٱللَّهُ لِيَذَرَ ٱلْمُؤْمِنِينَ عَلَىٰ مَآ أَنتُمْ عَلَيْهِ حَتَّىٰ يَمِيزَ ٱلْخَبِيثَ مِنَ ٱلطَّيِّبِ وَمَا كَانَ ٱللَّهُ

لِيُطْلِعَكُمْ عَلَى ٱلْغَيْبِ وَلَٰكِنَّ ٱللَّهَ يَجْتَبِى مِن رُّسُلِهِۦ مَن يَشَآءُ

"On no account will Allah leave the believers in the condition which you are in until He separates the evil from the good; nor is Allah going to make you acquainted with the unseen, but Allah chooses of His apostles whom He pleases..." (3:179)

ذِى قُوَّةٍ عِندَ ذِى ٱلْعَرْشِ مَكِينٍ ۝ مُّطَاعٍ ثَمَّ أَمِينٍ ۝ وَمَا صَاحِبُكُم بِمَجْنُونٍ ۝

وَلَقَدْ رَءَاهُ بِٱلْأُفُقِ ٱلْمُبِينِ ۝ وَمَا هُوَ عَلَى ٱلْغَيْبِ بِضَنِينٍ ۝

"The processor of strength, having an honorable place with the Lord of the Dominion, One (to be) obeyed, and faithful in trust. And your companion is not gone mad. And of a truth he saw himself on the clear horizon. Nor of the unseen is he a tenacious concealer." (81:20-24)

ذَٰلِكَ مِنْ أَنۢبَآءِ ٱلْغَيْبِ نُوحِيهِ إِلَيْكَ

"This is of the announcements relating to the unseen which We reveal to you..." (3:44)

From the above verses, it can be concluded that since the knowledge of unseen is itself restricted to the being of Almighty Allah and the way of access to unseen for human beings is closed, but the selected prophets are able to connect to the world of unseen through revelation and gain knowledge and learn about the realties of unseen.

On the whole it can be concluded from these verses that absolute unseen is restricted only to Almighty Allah since His being is unlimited and He has complete knowledge about seen and unseen world, so much so that even the prophets do not have this knowledge in the beginning, but since they have the capacity to receive revelation and get connected to the unseen world, through the assistance and grace of Almighty Allah they can maintain contact with unseen world and according to their own capacity and capability get access to the unending realities of the unseen world.

MIRACLE – A TESTIMONY OF PROPHETHOOD

Prophets claim to have connection with Almighty Allah and the unseen world and that they are appointed by God on the office of conveying His message to the people and to guide them to the path of religion. These claims are very great and people will not accept their statements without any reliable testimony. Therefore they should have evidence to prove the veracity of their claims. The greatest proof is the miracle of the prophets. Miracle is an extraordinary act which ordinary people are unable to perform. Prophets must have miracles in order to prove their extraordinary claims. So that the veracity of their claims is proved and the argument is exhausted. If it is not so how people would understand that they are true in their claims? And how can they distinguish the true prophets from false claimants of prophethood?

In view of the Holy Quran, it is necessary for divine prophets to display miracles, and this point is mentioned on numerous occasions. For example the staff of Prophet Musa (a), which used to be transformed into a python and swallowed the ropes of sorcerers; he stroke the staff on stone and springs of water gushed out from it; he stroked the staff on the surface of water and it split exposing a path through which the Bani Israel crossed to the opposite side. Another example is that of the talking of Prophet Isa (a) while he was yet an infant in a cradle;

his curing the born leper and raising the dead, giving life to the bird of clay and the cooling of the inferno for Prophet Ibrahim (a).

For example, pay attention to the following verses:

قَالَ إِن كُنتَ جِئْتَ بِـَٔايَةٖ فَأْتِ بِهَآ إِن كُنتَ مِنَ ٱلصَّٰدِقِينَ ۝ فَأَلْقَىٰ عَصَاهُ فَإِذَا هِيَ ثُعْبَانٞ مُّبِينٞ ۝ وَنَزَعَ يَدَهُۥ فَإِذَا هِيَ بَيْضَآءُ لِلنَّٰظِرِينَ ۝

"He said: If you have come with a sign, then bring it, if you are of the truthful ones. So he threw his rod, then lo! it was a clear serpent. And he drew forth his hand, and lo! it was white to the beholders." (7:106-108)

وَأَوْحَيْنَآ إِلَىٰ مُوسَىٰٓ أَنْ أَلْقِ عَصَاكَۖ فَإِذَا هِيَ تَلْقَفُ مَا يَأْفِكُونَ ۝

"And We revealed to Musa, saying: Cast your rod; then lo! it devoured the lies they told." (7:117)

وَإِذِ ٱسْتَسْقَىٰ مُوسَىٰ لِقَوْمِهِۦ فَقُلْنَا ٱضْرِب بِّعَصَاكَ ٱلْحَجَرَۖ فَٱنفَجَرَتْ مِنْهُ ٱثْنَتَا عَشْرَةَ عَيْنٗاۖ قَدْ عَلِمَ كُلُّ أُنَاسٖ مَّشْرَبَهُمْۖ كُلُواْ وَٱشْرَبُواْ مِن رِّزْقِ ٱللَّهِ وَلَا تَعْثَوْاْ فِي ٱلْأَرْضِ مُفْسِدِينَ ۝

"And when Musa prayed for drink for his people, We said: Strike the rock with your staff. So there gushed from it twelve springs; each tribe knew its drinking place: Eat and drink of the provisions of Allah and do not act corruptly in the land, making mischief." (2:60)

فَأَوْحَيْنَآ إِلَىٰ مُوسَىٰٓ أَنِ ٱضْرِب بِّعَصَاكَ ٱلْبَحْرَۖ فَٱنفَلَقَ فَكَانَ كُلُّ فِرْقٖ كَٱلطَّوْدِ ٱلْعَظِيمِ ۝ وَأَزْلَفْنَا ثَمَّ ٱلْءَاخَرِينَ ۝ وَأَنجَيْنَا مُوسَىٰ وَمَن مَّعَهُۥٓ أَجْمَعِينَ ۝ ثُمَّ أَغْرَقْنَا ٱلْءَاخَرِينَ ۝ إِنَّ فِي ذَٰلِكَ لَءَايَةٗۖ وَمَا كَانَ أَكْثَرُهُم مُّؤْمِنِينَ ۝

"Then We revealed to Musa: Strike the sea with your staff. So it had cloven asunder, and each part was like a huge mound. And We brought near, there, the others. And We saved Musa and those with him, all of them. Then We drowned the others. Most surely there is a sign in this, but most of them do not believe." *(26:63-67)*

قَالُوا۟ حَرِّقُوهُ وَٱنصُرُوٓا۟ ءَالِهَتَكُمْ إِن كُنتُمْ فَـٰعِلِينَ ۝ قُلْنَا يَـٰنَارُ كُونِى بَرْدًا وَسَلَـٰمًا عَلَىٰٓ إِبْرَٰهِيمَ ۝

"They said: Burn him and help your gods, if you are going to do (anything). We said: O fire! be a comfort and peace to Ibrahim..." *(21:68-69)*

From these verses and tens of others like it, it can be concluded that existence of miracles of prophets in the view of Quran is a fact and whoever considers Quran as a heavenly book, cannot deny the origin of miracles. Basically, Quran introduces itself as a miracle and says:

قُل لَّئِنِ ٱجْتَمَعَتِ ٱلْإِنسُ وَٱلْجِنُّ عَلَىٰٓ أَن يَأْتُوا۟ بِمِثْلِ هَـٰذَا ٱلْقُرْءَانِ لَا يَأْتُونَ بِمِثْلِهِۦ وَلَوْ كَانَ بَعْضُهُمْ لِبَعْضٍ ظَهِيرًا ۝

"Say: If men and jinn should combine together to bring the like of this Quran, they could not bring the like of it, though some of them were aiders of others." *(17:88)*

Definition of Miracle

Miracle is an extraordinary act performed through an unnatural and unknown way. In other words, law of causality is a complete rational law and Quran has also accepted it. That is why nothing comes into existence without a cause; so much so that miracles are also not without a cause.

Finally, the fact is that a phenomenon can be produced in two ways: natural and unnatural (miraculous); for example a staff can transform into a python in two ways:

Firstly: Through the channel of natural causes and factors; that is by the passage of time, natural actions and reactions, when the matter of the staff develops the capability to accept the being of the python. After that from the side of Almighty Allah the form and being of the python is added to it. In this case the python has come into being through natural causes and factors and no miracle has been employed.

Secondly: Through miracle. In this instance also the matter of the staff develops the capability of accepting the soul of the python not through natural actions and reactions, on the contrary it is instantly through the spiritual power of the prophet and his absolute intention that such a capability has developed in the matter of the staff. At that moment the soul of the python is added to it by Almighty Allah and it is transformed into a real python. Therefore, in case of a miracle also the phenomenon does not occurs without a cause; at the most its natural cause is not recognized; on the contrary it occurs as a result of divine will and unnatural and extraordinary causes. From this aspect, it is named as a miracle and it is a testimony to the veracity of the prophet.

Whose act is a Miracle?

Is the miracle a directly action of Almighty Allah without any intermediary or it is the act of the prophet only as a demand of circumstances? Or is it the act of the prophet himself that he performs with his own will?

In some verses, the Holy Quran has related miracle to the prophets; for example: He says in the words of Prophet Isa (a):

$$\text{أَنِّي قَدْ جِئْتُكُم بِآيَةٍ مِّن رَّبِّكُمْ أَنِّي أَخْلُقُ لَكُم مِّنَ ٱلطِّينِ كَهَيْـَٔةِ ٱلطَّيْرِ فَأَنفُخُ فِيهِ فَيَكُونُ طَيْرًۢا بِإِذْنِ ٱللَّهِ وَأُبْرِئُ ٱلْأَكْمَهَ وَٱلْأَبْرَصَ وَأُحْىِ ٱلْمَوْتَىٰ بِإِذْنِ ٱللَّهِ وَأُنَبِّئُكُم بِمَا تَأْكُلُونَ وَمَا تَدَّخِرُونَ فِى بُيُوتِكُمْ}$$

"That I have come to you with a sign from your Lord, that I determine for you out of dust like the form of a bird, then I breathe into it and it becomes a bird with Allah's permission and I heal the blind and the leprous, and bring the dead to life with Allah's permission and I inform you of what you should eat and what you should store in your houses." (3:49)

In Surah Maidah, He says:

$$\text{وَإِذْ تَخْلُقُ مِنَ ٱلطِّينِ كَهَيْـَٔةِ ٱلطَّيْرِ بِإِذْنِى فَتَنفُخُ فِيهَا فَتَكُونُ طَيْرًۢا بِإِذْنِى وَتُبْرِئُ ٱلْأَكْمَهَ وَٱلْأَبْرَصَ بِإِذْنِى وَإِذْ تُخْرِجُ ٱلْمَوْتَىٰ بِإِذْنِى}$$

"...and when you determined out of clay a thing like the form of a bird by My permission, then you breathed into it and it became a bird by My permission, and you healed the blind and the leprous by My permission; and when you brought forth the dead by My permission." (5:110)

With regard to Prophet Musa (a), He says:

$$\text{قَالَ إِن كُنتَ جِئْتَ بِـَٔايَةٍ فَأْتِ بِهَآ إِن كُنتَ مِنَ ٱلصَّـٰدِقِينَ ۝ فَأَلْقَىٰ عَصَاهُ فَإِذَا هِىَ ثُعْبَانٌ مُّبِينٌ ۝ وَنَزَعَ يَدَهُۥ فَإِذَا هِىَ بَيْضَآءُ لِلنَّـٰظِرِينَ ۝}$$

"He said: If you have come with a sign, then bring it, if you are of the truthful ones. So he threw his rod, then lo! it was a clear serpent. And he drew forth his hand, and lo! it was white to the beholders." (7:106-108)

In some verses, the miracle has also been related to Almighty Allah; for example:

$$\text{وَظَلَّلْنَا عَلَيْكُمُ ٱلْغَمَامَ وَأَنزَلْنَا عَلَيْكُمُ ٱلْمَنَّ وَٱلسَّلْوَىٰ}$$

"And We made the clouds to give shade over you and We sent to you manna and quails." (2:57)

In any case, it can generally be concluded from the verses that miracle is the direct act of the prophet, which is performed through his will and intention; but the prophet is not independent in its performance; instead, his action is subject to the permission and help of Almighty Allah. Although will and intention of the prophet is a means to causes, but the one who has given reality to it is Almighty Allah. That is why in most verses, the performance of miracle is related to the prophet, but it is made conditional to His leave. In one verse, this point is mentioned with more clarity:

$$\text{وَمَا كَانَ لِرَسُولٍ أَن يَأْتِىَ بِـَٔايَةٍ إِلَّا بِإِذْنِ ٱللَّهِ ۚ فَإِذَا جَآءَ أَمْرُ ٱللَّهِ قُضِىَ بِٱلْحَقِّ وَخَسِرَ هُنَالِكَ ٱلْمُبْطِلُونَ ۝}$$

"...and it was not meet for an apostle that he should bring a sign except with Allah's permission, but when the command of Allah came, judgment was given with truth, and those who treated (it) as a lie were lost." (40:78)

Difference between Miracle and Magic

At this point the question arises: If prophet from the aspect of miracle performs an extraordinary act that others cannot do, the sorcerer also performs amazing acts which others are unable to do. Thus what is the difference between miracle and magic? And how can one be satisfied that the act of the claimant of prophethood is a miracle and not magic? In reply to this question, we shall mention some differences:

Firstly: In magic, the occurrence which takes place is not real; on the contrary the sorcerer influences the senses and perception of people in order to display a non-factual and unreal happening. Thus in the story of Prophet Musa (a), the magicians threw ropes, staffs and other instruments of magic before the people and by magic performed acts so that in the view of people they appeared as pythons and snakes, who came into being and moved about here and there horrifying the audience, while in fact there were no pythons and snakes there. Therefore Quran says:

قَالَ أَلْقُوا۟ فَلَمَّآ أَلْقَوْا۟ سَحَرُوٓا۟ أَعْيُنَ ٱلنَّاسِ وَٱسْتَرْهَبُوهُمْ وَجَآءُو بِسِحْرٍ عَظِيمٍ ﴿١١٦﴾

"He said: Cast. So when they cast, they deceived the people's eyes and frightened them, and they produced a mighty enchantment." (7:116)

But in case of miracle, a factual and natural matter comes into existence. In the story of Prophet Musa (a), his staff really changed into a python and it really swallowed up the magic of the magicians. Almighty Allah told Prophet Musa (a):

قُلْنَا لَا تَخَفْ إِنَّكَ أَنتَ ٱلْأَعْلَىٰ ﴿٦٨﴾ وَأَلْقِ مَا فِى يَمِينِكَ تَلْقَفْ مَا صَنَعُوٓا۟ إِنَّمَا صَنَعُوا۟ كَيْدُ سَٰحِرٍ وَلَا يُفْلِحُ ٱلسَّاحِرُ حَيْثُ أَتَىٰ ﴿٦٩﴾ فَأُلْقِىَ ٱلسَّحَرَةُ سُجَّدًا قَالُوٓا۟ ءَامَنَّا بِرَبِّ هَٰرُونَ وَمُوسَىٰ ﴿٧٠﴾

"We said: Fear not, surely you shall be the uppermost, and cast down what is in your right hand; it shall devour what they have wrought; they have wrought

only the plan of a magician, and the magician shall not be successful wheresoever he may come from. And the magicians were cast down making obeisance; they said: We believe in the Lord of Harun and Musa." (20:68-70)

That is why when the magicians saw that the python of Prophet Musa (a) has swallowed the instruments of their magic, they understood that the act of Musa (a) was a miracle and that it was totally different from their act. Therefore they surrendered before it and embraced faith.

Secondly: The sorcerer is needful of special acts for his job or he has to use some recitations and magic words; or to draw some figures etc. and write some charms. But no such thing is required for magic; only the will and desire of the prophet is enough to perform that act through the help of Almighty Allah.

Thirdly: Miracle is never defeated; that is when the prophet desires something it definitely turns into a reality and no human power can prevent its occurrence or that he should be able to invalidate it after its occurrence, since it has originated from divine power; but such is not the case with regard to magic; because it is possible that a magician superior to him can defeat him or a prophet can invalidate it as happened in the story of Prophet Musa (a).

Fourthly: Magic is considered as a science and a craft; on the contrary showing miracles cannot be taught and learnt. An ordinary person can learn magic through training and practice and he does not need to have faith in Almighty Allah or develop connection with Him; but the power of miracle is a divine bestowal and is not obtained through learning and practice and the performer of miracle is in possession of extensively lofty faith and has a deep connection with Almighty Allah.

METHODS TO RECOGNIZE THE PROPHET

The following methods may be employed in order to recognize true prophets and to certify their claims:

1. Miracle: Asking for a miracle is the best and the most satisfactory way to recognize the prophet. If the claimant of prophethood is in possession of miracle or miracles to prove the veracity of his claim, its existence is absolute proof like witnessing or a reliable and definite report and hence his prophethood is proved.

2. Information given by Past Prophets: In case the previous prophet, whose prophethood had been proved, gives information about the advent of the prophet after himself and mentions his distinctive qualities perfectly, the prophethood of the latter would also be proved as happened in case of the Prophet of Islam. The past prophets gave glad tidings of his arrival, which were recorded in their books. Quran has mentioned this same point in the words of Prophet Isa (a):

وَإِذْ قَالَ عِيسَى ٱبْنُ مَرْيَمَ يَنبَنِىٓ إِسْرَٰٓءِيلَ إِنِّى رَسُولُ ٱللَّهِ إِلَيْكُم مُّصَدِّقًا لِّمَا بَيْنَ يَدَىَّ مِنَ ٱلتَّوْرَىٰةِ وَمُبَشِّرًۢا بِرَسُولٍ يَأْتِى مِنۢ بَعْدِى ٱسْمُهُۥٓ أَحْمَدُ

"And when Isa son of Maryam said: O children of Israel! surely I am the apostle of Allah to you,

verifying that which is before me of the Taurat and giving the good news of an Apostle who will come after me, his name being Ahmad..." (61:6)

3. Study of the text of the laws and programs of religion of the prophet: If an intellectual or researcher studies in detail religious cognitions, laws, rules and programs of religion and its different dimensions without prejudice and evaluates them, he can discover the value and comprehensiveness of that religion. Whether the view of the laws of that religion are according to the criterion of reason and its rules have really complied with the actual needs of the society and that it defends individual rights and social units of the community and observes social justice; and assures the success of man in the world and the hereafter. And by observing its good ethics, which advise its followers to keep away from bad manners etc. he discovers the truthfulness and perfection of that religion and in this way it supports and verifies the prophethood of the prophet.

At this point it is necessary to mention two points: Firstly: Such minute research and indeed all aspects of reformation of people would be limited and cannot become the responsibility of the people. Secondly: In case of certainty, it can be relied upon only within limit of contexts and testimonies, but it cannot be presented as decisive proof. In any case, it does not make us needless of the proof of miracle.

4. Study of life, character and behavior of the claimant of prophethood: If the claimant of prophethood is a person whose trustworthiness, honesty and truthfulness is proved to others and there is no weak point in his internal and external character and he practices what he preaches,

he would be supported and verified by the people with regard to the claim of prophethood also. But this topic also would be considered only as a confirmation and not an absolute proof and lawful argument.

REVELATION

According to the dictionary meaning, revelation is the conveying of a message in a secret manner to another. In Islamic terminology it is defined as the dialogue of Almighty Allah with the prophets. They were claiming to have a special connection with God and that Almighty Allah speaks to them and conveys His messages to the people through them. They claimed that they can hear the statements of Almighty Allah and see realities in the unseen world and that they have been appointed on behalf of God so that they may convey His messages to the people.

Knowledge of the prophets is obtained through the channel of revelation and it is absolutely opposed to our acquisition of knowledge. We have three kinds of knowledge: Knowledge of senses, knowledge gained through generalities and internal perceptions and realizations. Knowledge of senses is obtained directly from the five senses. The senses also have a role in the knowledge of generalities, because their parts previously were realized through the channel of these senses. After that the generalities are separated from them. The third type is through the inner senses, like: the perception of pain, hunger, thirst, happiness and sorrow. All our knowledge is obtained through the channel of inner or outer senses directly or indirectly. But revelation is not a part of any of them and is having no similarity to them.

Prophets witness the reality in the unseen world and hear the words of God, but not with these eyes and ears. In this instance, knowledge is transferred from Almighty Allah to the heart of the prophets through revelation and at that moment it becomes apparent. Exactly opposed to it is ordinary knowledge which in the beginning is obtained through senses and in the end it enters our selves and hearts. The Quran has also interpreted revelation in this manner:

وَإِنَّهُ لَتَنزِيلُ رَبِّ ٱلْعَٰلَمِينَ ۞ نَزَلَ بِهِ ٱلرُّوحُ ٱلْأَمِينُ ۞ عَلَىٰ قَلْبِكَ لِتَكُونَ مِنَ ٱلْمُنذِرِينَ ۞ بِلِسَانٍ عَرَبِيٍّ مُّبِينٍ ۞

"And most surely this is a revelation from the Lord of the worlds. The Faithful Spirit has descended with it. Upon your heart that you may be of the warners, In plain Arabic language." (26:192-195)

قُلْ مَن كَانَ عَدُوًّا لِّجِبْرِيلَ فَإِنَّهُ نَزَّلَهُ عَلَىٰ قَلْبِكَ

"Say: Whoever is the enemy of Jibraeel- for surely he revealed it to your heart..." (Surah Baqarah 2:97)

It is mentioned in *Tafsir Ruhul Bayan* that:

Whenever revelation descended on Prophet Muhammad (ṣ), it first descended upon his heart as he was extremely thirsty for it. At that moment his heart absorbed it. Then he understood it through his heart and heard it and this is in the meaning of coming down from a height and this is the status of the special ones.[1]

The late Allamah Tabatabai (q) has said: Heart denotes the self of man, which has the power of perception,

---

[1] *Tafsir Ruhul Bayan*, Vol. 6, Pg. 306

perhaps the reason why Quran has mentioned:

$$نَزَلَ بِهِ الرُّوحُ الْأَمِينُ ۝ عَلَىٰ قَلْبِكَ$$

"The Faithful Spirit has descended with it. Upon your heart..." (26:192-195)

And did not say: "upon you", which indicates the comprehensiveness of Quran from the side of the Holy Prophet (s) and also whatever he received from the soul was his noble self without his conscious perception having any interference in it.

Therefore, he hears whatever is revealed to him without the intervention of his eyes and ears. Because if his seeing and hearing had been through the apparent eyes and ears, everything he heard would be shared by others; that is whatever he sees, people also see it, while the fact is that traditional reports have refuted this meaning absolutely.[1]

That is why, the knowledge of prophets, which is obtained through revelation, is not like obtained knowledge learned through perception and human thinking, on the contrary it is of a higher type, whose essence is not clear to us. It is a type of secret and hidden understanding and errors and doubts cannot enter it.

From some verses, it is learnt that revelation takes place in one of the following three ways:

First method: Almighty Allah reveals matters directly on the heart of the prophet.

---

[1] *Al-Mizan*, Vol. 15, Pg. 345

Revelation

Second method: Matters are sent down to another place and the prophet obtains from there, like in the case of the conversation of Prophet Musa (a) at Mount Tur through the tree. The Holy Quran says:

فَلَمَّآ أَتَنهَا نُودِىَ مِن شَطِئِ ٱلۡوَادِ ٱلۡأَيۡمَنِ فِى ٱلۡبُقۡعَةِ ٱلۡمُبَٰرَكَةِ مِنَ ٱلشَّجَرَةِ

"And when he came to it, a voice was uttered from the right side of the valley in the blessed spot of the bush..." (28:30)

Third method: Some points are revealed through the angel of revelation (Jibraeel) on the heart of the prophet.

These three methods are mentioned in the Holy Quran when Almighty Allah says:

وَمَا كَانَ لِبَشَرٍ أَن يُكَلِّمَهُ ٱللَّهُ إِلَّا وَحۡيًا أَوۡ مِن وَرَآئِ حِجَابٍ أَوۡ يُرۡسِلَ رَسُولًا فَيُوحِىَ بِإِذۡنِهِۦ مَا يَشَآءُ إِنَّهُۥ عَلِىٌّ حَكِيمٌ ۝

"And it is not for any mortal that Allah should speak to him except by revelation or from behind a veil, or by sending a messenger and revealing by His permission what He pleases, Surely He is High, wise." (42:51)

But it should be known that in every method, the dialogue is only with Almighty Allah and that is why in most verses, revelation is related to Almighty Allah, but through a medium of cause and effects, one of them being Jibraeel.

Hence, these three methods of revelation should be interpreted in the effect of psychological conditions of the prophet and various divine emotions. In this case, sometimes the ethereal soul of the prophet rises up to the position of Jibraeel and he hears the divine revelation from him. But he does not see himself till he himself saw

Jibraeel with his eyes. Sometimes the progress of his soul is to the limit that he hears the speech of Almighty Allah at a designated place like a tree etc. In that case also, his soul rises up such a level that he sees the medium and hears the dialogue directly from Almighty Allah.

Allamah Tabatabai (q) has mentioned the same point when he says:

The proof of veil (*Hijab*) or the conveyer of the message at the time of speaking does not use the medium of revelation, because revelation like his other characters is not without a medium, only the pivot is the attention of the one who is addressed. Thus if the prophet were to see through which he is getting divine revelation, and through this medium he veils the statement and message, which has come to him from Almighty Allah; like the medium of angel, in that case revelation is on that angel. Thus when the prophet looks at God, the revelation will be from Almighty Allah. Although there is also a medium, but the prophet pays no attention to it.[1]

That is why revelation is a kind of a hidden and inner understanding and perception, which the apparent and hidden perceptions and logical prefaces have no intervention in. On the contrary, it is directly inspired to the heart of the prophet. Since the self of the prophet has reached to the highest level of humanity it has the capacity to obtain such information; but revelation is not ordinary knowledge; it is an extraordinary matter. Therefore people demand miracle from the prophets. The latter also in order to prove the veracity of their claim, perform miracles in situations that demand it.

---

[1] *Al-Mizan*, Vol. 14, Pg. 150

NUMBER OF PROPHETS

Throughout the history, a large number of prophets were sent to guide human beings. His Eminence, Adam (a) was the first of the divine prophets and The Holy Prophet Muhammad (s) was the last of them. The exact number of prophets is not known, but in some traditions their number is mentioned as 124000. Some prophets were having special and particular laws and some others were not having special code of laws; on the contrary they promoted the Shariah of the previous prophet. Some of them brought scriptures and some others did not bring any books. Sometimes there were more than one prophet in a single town or city, who fulfilled the duties of prophethood.

It is narrated from Abu Zar that one day he asked the Messenger of Allah (s): How many prophets are there in all? He replied: One hundred and twenty four thousand. He then asked: How many of them were messenger prophets? He replied: Three hundred thirteen from the above group. He asked: Who was the first of them? He replied: Adam. He asked: Was he a messenger prophet? He replied: Yes, Almighty Allah created him with His own hands and blew His spirit into him. At that moment the Holy Prophet (s) said: O Abu Zar:

There were four from the Syriac prophets: Adam, Sheeth, and Ukhnuh, who is also called Idris and who was the first to write and Nuh. Four of them were Arabs: Hud, Salih, Shuaib and your prophet, Muhammad. The first prophet among Bani Israel was Musa and the last of them was Isa and they were in all six hundred prophets.

Abu Zar asked: O Messenger of Allah (s), how many heavenly scriptures descended? He replied: One hundred and four, of which Almighty Allah revealed to Sheeth fifty scrolls, thirty on Idris and twenty on Ibrahim. He also revealed Taurat, Injeel, Zabur and Quran.[1]

Five great divine prophets brought new sets of laws (Shariah) and they are known as *Ulul Azm* prophets. They were: Nuh, Ibrahim, Musa, Isa and Muhammad (s).

Ismail Jofi has narrated from Imam Muhammad Baqir (a) that he said:

The *Ulul Azm* prophets are five in number: Nuh, Ibrahim, Musa, Isa and Muhammad (s).[2]

We do not have detailed information about the names of all the prophets; in books of history also only some of their names are mentioned. In the Holy Quran, twenty-six of them are mentioned by names: They are: Adam, Nuh, Idris, Hud, Salih, Ibrahim, Lut, Ismail, Al-Yasa, Zulkifl, Ilyas, Ayyub, Yunus, Ishaq, Yaqub, Yusuf, Shuaib, Musa, Harun, Dawood, Sulaiman, Zakariya, Yahya, Ismail the keeper of his word, Isa and Muhammad (s).

---

[1] *Biharul Anwar*, Vol. 11, Pg. 32

[2] *Biharul Anwar*, Vol. 11, Pg. 32

AIMS OF THE PROPHETS

Prophets in the capacity of their appointment by Almighty Allah followed some aims, which are mentioned in verses of the Holy Quran and traditions, but all of them could be summed up in two general points:

First aim: Calling the attention of the people to the value and significance of their spiritual life and their guidance to matters, which results in the perfection of self and proximity to God; and guarantees the success of the hereafter. Similarly they explain and warn about the causes and reasons for decline of the self and misfortune in the world of the hereafter. In this regard, pay attention to some important points as follows:

1. Recognition and faith in the One and only God, proofs of the qualities of perfection for that Holy being and purifying Him from the defective traits was the basis of the call of the prophets and the first of their proposals and most of the verses of the Holy Quran are also in connection with this subject:

2. Calling the attention of the people to faith in resurrection and life after death and belief in Paradise and bounties of the hereafter; as well as Hell and its chastisements was a part of their message. Prophets in proving the world of the hereafter emphasize on its rewards and punishments and a large number of verses of Quran are also about this.

3. Testifying the past prophets and calling the people to accept the new laws and Shariah and to follow his own prophethood.

These three acts were the basis of the call of the prophets. The Holy Prophet (ṣ) in his call to his relatives said:

"Praise is only for Almighty Allah. I praise Him and ask help from Him and I have faith and reliance on Him. And I witness that there is no god except Him and that He has no associate. Then he said: The leader does not lie to his followers. By Allah, except whom there is no god, I am the messenger sent especially to you and generally to all the people. I swear by Allah, just as you sleep you would die and you will rise up just as you wake up. You will have to account for your deeds as a result of which you will either get everlasting Paradise or everlasting Hell."[1]

4. To motivate people to assume good manners and ethics and to warn them from improper acts. By explaining the worldly and other worldly effects of good ethics, prophets invited the people to good behavior and by explaining to them bad consequences of evil behavior they warned them. Therefore purifying and disciplining of the selves can be considered as an important aim of the prophets; just as Almighty Allah says:

لَقَدْ مَنَّ ٱللَّهُ عَلَى ٱلْمُؤْمِنِينَ إِذْ بَعَثَ فِيهِمْ رَسُولًا مِنْ أَنفُسِهِمْ يَتْلُواْ عَلَيْهِمْ ءَايَٰتِهِۦ وَيُزَكِّيهِمْ وَيُعَلِّمُهُمُ ٱلْكِتَٰبَ وَٱلْحِكْمَةَ وَإِن كَانُواْ مِن قَبْلُ لَفِى ضَلَٰلٍ مُّبِينٍ ﴿١٦٤﴾

---

[1] *Al-Kamil fit Tarikh*, Vol. 2, Pg. 41

> *"Certainly Allah conferred a benefit upon the believers when He raised among them an Apostle from among themselves, reciting to them His communications and purifying them, and teaching them the Book and the wisdom, although before that they were surely in manifest error."* (3:164)

The Holy Prophet (s) said:

> *"I advise you to follow good manners and ethics as Almighty Allah has raised me for the same purpose."*[1]

Imam Ali (a) has narrated from the Messenger of Allah (s) that he said:

> *"I have been sent for the perfection of morals and improving the manners (of people)."*[2]

5. Motivating people to the worship of one God and submission to His commands. Prophets have introduced a number of different types of worship acts and they consider them as causes of perfection of the self and gaining proximity to Almighty Allah. Their performance is very much effective in the success of man in the life hereafter. So much so that it is mentioned that the aim of creation of man is not but the worship of God as mentioned in the following verse:

وَلَقَدْ بَعَثْنَا فِى كُلِّ أُمَّةٍ رَسُولًا أَنِ اعْبُدُوا اللَّهَ وَاجْتَنِبُوا الطَّاغُوتَ

> *"And certainly We raised in every nation an apostle saying: Serve Allah and shun the Shaitan."* (16:36)

وَمَا خَلَقْتُ الْجِنَّ وَالْإِنسَ إِلَّا لِيَعْبُدُونِ ۝

---

[1] *Biharul Anwar*, Vol. 69, Pg. 375
[2] *Biharul Anwar*, Vol. 69, Pg. 405

"And I have not created the jinn and the men except that they should serve Me." (51:56)

By showing such a program to the people, the prophets called them to get assured success in the hereafter.

Second aim: Reforming the social conditions and worldly life of people. The prophets also paid full attention to reforming the social and economic circumstances of the people. They called people to acquisition of knowledge, gaining from natural resources and making efforts and putting in hard work as well as to observe justice; on the other hand they warned about injustice and oppression. They conveyed to the people rules and regulations to prevent injustice and oppression and to establish social justice; they also described the rights and duties as well as penalties and punishments in order to usher complete governance and they also struggled to establish this system. They confronted injustice and tyranny and supported the weak and the deprived.

By studying and researching the laws of Islam, it becomes absolutely clear that the religion of Islam is perfectly concerned about reforming the worldly affairs and social conditions of the people.

From some verses, it is also concluded that it was one of the aims of the prophets. For example it is said in Quran that:

لَقَدْ أَرْسَلْنَا رُسُلَنَا بِٱلْبَيِّنَٰتِ وَأَنزَلْنَا مَعَهُمُ ٱلْكِتَٰبَ وَٱلْمِيزَانَ لِيَقُومَ ٱلنَّاسُ بِٱلْقِسْطِ وَأَنزَلْنَا ٱلْحَدِيدَ فِيهِ بَأْسٌ شَدِيدٌ وَمَنَٰفِعُ لِلنَّاسِ وَلِيَعْلَمَ ٱللَّهُ مَن يَنصُرُهُۥ وَرُسُلَهُۥ بِٱلْغَيْبِ إِنَّ ٱللَّهَ قَوِىٌّ عَزِيزٌ ۝

"Certainly We sent Our apostles with clear arguments, and sent down with them the Book and the balance that men may conduct themselves with equity; and We have made the iron, wherein is great violence and advantages to men, and that Allah may know who helps Him and His apostles in the secret; surely Allah is Strong, Mighty." (57:25)

In another verse it is said:

$$\text{كَانَ ٱلنَّاسُ أُمَّةً وَٰحِدَةً فَبَعَثَ ٱللَّهُ ٱلنَّبِيِّـۧنَ مُبَشِّرِينَ وَمُنذِرِينَ وَأَنزَلَ مَعَهُمُ ٱلۡكِتَٰبَ بِٱلۡحَقِّ لِيَحۡكُمَ بَيۡنَ ٱلنَّاسِ فِيمَا ٱخۡتَلَفُواْ فِيهِۚ وَمَا ٱخۡتَلَفَ فِيهِ إِلَّا ٱلَّذِينَ أُوتُوهُ مِنۢ بَعۡدِ مَا جَآءَتۡهُمُ ٱلۡبَيِّنَٰتُ بَغۡيَۢا بَيۡنَهُمۡۖ فَهَدَى ٱللَّهُ ٱلَّذِينَ ءَامَنُواْ لِمَا ٱخۡتَلَفُواْ فِيهِ مِنَ ٱلۡحَقِّ بِإِذۡنِهِۦۗ وَٱللَّهُ يَهۡدِي مَن يَشَآءُ إِلَىٰ صِرَٰطٖ مُّسۡتَقِيمٍ}$$

"(All) people are a single nation; so Allah raised prophets as bearers of good news and as warners, and He revealed with them the Book with truth, that it might judge between people in that in which they differed; and none but the very people who were given it differed about it after clear arguments had come to them, revolting among themselves; so Allah has guided by His will those who believe to the truth about which they differed and Allah guides whom He pleases to the right path." (2:213)

The final aim of the prophets

We say that prophets in their divine office follow two general aims: One is the recognition of God and His worship and proximity, which is related to the spiritual life and success of the hereafter of human beings and the second is the establishment of justice and equity and negation of injustice and prejudice, which is related to the worldly life of man.

Now the question arises that whether the prophets were inclined to two aims in their messengership? That is, did they pursue the above two aims separately? Or did considered one of them as primary and the other as secondary? If we suppose the latter, which is the primary aim and which is the secondary? At this point, there are a few possibilities:

1. Some are of the opinion that the main aim of the prophets is to assure the worldly success of man and establishment of justice and equity. The prophets came with the aim to restrain differences and oppositions and to make human life peaceful and prosperous. If with regard to the need of recognition and worship of Allah they stressed on resurrection, rewards and punishments of the hereafter, moral values like justice, favor, sacrifice, forgiveness, and defense of the deprived and weak, it was with the aim that they should maintain social justice and that it should be effective in negating injustice and prejudice. It is said: Unity of view and recognition of God is in itself of no benefit and whether we recognize God or not, whether we worship or do not worship, it is of no use to Allah. They should be considered as mediums of social unity and establishment of a just society.

2. Researches and real scholars of Islam, consider training of selves and reformation of spiritual life of man as the final aim of the prophets. Therefore in order to reach this aim, they consider theoretical monotheism, faith in resurrection and prophethood, worship and submission before the One God, purification and discipline of the self and following good ethics as necessary and effective. We mention some points to support this view:

A) It is concluded from Islamic philosophy, verses of Quran and traditions that man with regard to the ethereal soul is an abstract being and is superior to matter; he is everlasting and never annihilated or destroyed by death. On the contrary, he is transferred from this world to the world of the hereafter, so that he may see the good and bad consequences of his deeds. Man in the dimension of his ethereal soul is moving to perfection; by nature he is searching for God and perfection, he struggles for success and well being in the recognition of God and in His worship and proximity and his original life will also be like the spiritual and other worldly life.

B) In some verses and traditions, it is explained that life and worldly affairs do not have any value and the real and valuable life of man is the spiritual life of the hereafter. For example:

اَلْمَالُ وَٱلْبَنُونَ زِينَةُ ٱلْحَيَوٰةِ ٱلدُّنْيَا وَٱلْبَٰقِيَٰتُ ٱلصَّٰلِحَٰتُ خَيْرٌ عِندَ رَبِّكَ ثَوَابًا وَخَيْرٌ أَمَلًا ﴿٤٦﴾

"Wealth and children are an adornment of the life of this world; and the ever-abiding, the good works, are better with your Lord in reward and better in expectation." (18:46)

ٱعْلَمُوٓا۟ أَنَّمَا ٱلْحَيَوٰةُ ٱلدُّنْيَا لَعِبٌ وَلَهْوٌ وَزِينَةٌ وَتَفَاخُرٌۢ بَيْنَكُمْ وَتَكَاثُرٌ فِى ٱلْأَمْوَٰلِ وَٱلْأَوْلَٰدِ كَمَثَلِ غَيْثٍ أَعْجَبَ ٱلْكُفَّارَ نَبَاتُهُۥ ثُمَّ يَهِيجُ فَتَرَىٰهُ مُصْفَرًّا ثُمَّ يَكُونُ حُطَٰمًا وَفِى ٱلْءَاخِرَةِ عَذَابٌ شَدِيدٌ وَمَغْفِرَةٌ مِّنَ ٱللَّهِ وَرِضْوَٰنٌ وَمَا ٱلْحَيَوٰةُ ٱلدُّنْيَآ إِلَّا مَتَٰعُ ٱلْغُرُورِ ﴿٢٠﴾ سَابِقُوٓا۟ إِلَىٰ مَغْفِرَةٍ مِّن رَّبِّكُمْ وَجَنَّةٍ عَرْضُهَا كَعَرْضِ ٱلسَّمَآءِ وَٱلْأَرْضِ أُعِدَّتْ لِلَّذِينَ ءَامَنُوا۟ بِٱللَّهِ وَرُسُلِهِۦ ذَٰلِكَ فَضْلُ ٱللَّهِ يُؤْتِيهِ مَن يَشَآءُ وَٱللَّهُ ذُو ٱلْفَضْلِ ٱلْعَظِيمِ ﴿٢١﴾

> *"Know that this world's life is only sport and play and gaiety and boasting among yourselves, and a vying in the multiplication of wealth and children, like the rain, whose causing the vegetation to grow, pleases the husbandmen, then it withers away so that you will see it become yellow, then it becomes dried up and broken down; and in the hereafter is a severe chastisement and (also) forgiveness from Allah and (His) pleasure; and this world's life is naught but means of deception. Hasten to forgiveness from your Lord and to a garden the extensiveness of which is as the extensiveness of the heaven and the earth; it is prepared for those who believe in Allah and His apostles; that is the grace of Allah: He gives it to whom He pleases, and Allah is the Lord of mighty grace." (57:20-21)*

وَمَا أُوتِيتُم مِّن شَيْءٍ فَمَتَاعُ ٱلْحَيَوٰةِ ٱلدُّنْيَا وَزِينَتُهَا وَمَا عِندَ ٱللَّهِ خَيْرٌ وَأَبْقَىٰ أَفَلَا تَعْقِلُونَ ۝

> *"And whatever things you have been given are only a provision of this world's life and its adornment, and whatever is with Allah is better and more lasting; do you not then understand?" (28:60)*

In numerous traditions, this world is mentioned as a place of short stay and a station on the journey and the harvest field of the hereafter and that the everlasting life of the hereafter should benefit from it. For example, Imam Ali (a) said:

> *"Know that this world, which you have started to covet and in which you are interested, and which sometimes enrages you and sometimes pleases you, is not your (permanent) abode, nor the place of your stay for which you might have been created, nor one to which you have been invited."*[1]

---

[1] *Nahjul Balagha*, Sermon 173

In the same way, he said:

> *"Certainly this world has not been made a place of permanent stay for you. But it has been created as a pathway in order that you may take from it the provisions of your (good) actions for the permanent house (in Paradise)."*[1]

And he said:

> *"O people! The world is a place of transient stay and the hereafter is the place of permanent stay. Thus you should take advantage from the temporal place for the place of permanent stay. Do not raise the veils from those who know your secrets. Take out your hearts from the world before your bodies are taken out of it. Thus you will be tested in the world and you are created for something other than it."*[2]

From these verses, and traditions and their like it can be concluded that the actual life of man in the view of Islam is the spiritual life and life in the hereafter. And the life of the world is a medium of guaranteeing the success of the hereafter. That is why, it can be concluded that the final aim of the prophets also was to entrust to man, ways of gaining divine proximity, perfection and attainment of success and salvation; as they had learnt from Almighty Allah. Any other person cannot introduce such a method. Prophets introduced faith in God, resurrection, prophethood; worship of One God and taught that attaining good ethics is the only way to salvation.

---

[1] *Nahjul Balagha*, Sermon 132

[2] *Nahjul Balagha*, Saying 203

That is why, the second view is supported and the first view; that is the reformation of livelihood of people is disproved to be the final aim of the prophets as also opposed by verses and traditions.

But our aim is not that prophets paid no attention to reform the worldly life of man and to establish justice and equity and to oppose injustice, prejudice and differences. On the contrary, in order to attain these aims also they struggled as much as was possible. They introduced this same topic as a genuine value and one of the best channels of perfection of self and proximity of God. They considered efforts and service for the people and observance of justice, provided they are accompanied with sincerity, as the best worship acts. Since through this the social life of man is possible and through this may be achieved the purification and training of selves as well the worship of the One God.

This is a perfect refutation for one who says: Prophets were dualist in their aims and they paid equal attention to the affairs of the world and the hereafter as explained by them. Because the world in the view of the prophets was only having the value of a preface; that is, it was the harvest field of the hereafter. According to them it is possible to gain spiritual perfection and success for the hereafter in this world. Therefore the prophets did not consider hereafter to be absolutely divorced from this world. On the contrary, they tried make worldly affairs as means to perfect the soul and to secure success in the Hereafter.

TWO WORLD VIEWS

How do you view the world? How do you consider man as a phenomenon? What is your view with regard to man and the world? In reply to these questions, two totally opposite views exist: the divine view and the materialistic view: In other words: the religious world view and the materialistic world view.

Materialistic world view

The supporters of this type of view consider the world to be permanent and existence to have come about without any aim or intention. In this view, the world is a collection having no particular aim. On the contrary, it is shaped from material elements tangled with each other without any aim, and they all are vain and aimless. Within this great collection, man is also an aimless and confused existence marching towards annihilation. He does not have any motive and his end is despair, darkness and annihilation. He does not have any refuge or hope and he lives a life of darkness and horror.

The life of man is also according to the materialistic world view, vain and aimless. There is no one to whom man is answerable, no being who may be aware and higher to him and who may well know the good and bad of man and recognizes his behavior and who punishes or rewards him. And no absolute criterion exists to assess the deeds of man and his good and bad character...

Religious world view

In the religious world view, the present world is not permanent. On the contrary, it is created and it is dependant. In this view, the world is a creation, created on the basis of a minute accounting for continuity, arrangement and special compatibility for a designated aim and the world is dependant on the power of a powerful creator; forceful intention and a wise being, who is also powerful and is giving it continuous support and protection.

In the religious view, nothing in the world is vain and aimless. And among all the beings, man is having an excellence and has a higher aim that he pursues throughout his life. His end is not despair and hopelessness; on the contrary, it is hope and eagerness. He is a being, which cannot be annihilated; who is traveling in this temporal on his way to the permanent world of the hereafter. In the religious world view, man is answerable before his beneficent and merciful creator. He is having a great answerability before his God, as He has created him with free will and allotted duties to him.

Religious world view believes that man is having a creator who is seeing and aware. He is the witness of all his actions all the time, and He rewards the doers of good deeds and punishes the wrong doers.

World view of the prophets

The view of the prophets about man and the world is divine. Prophets consider the worldly phenomena to be dependant and needful. They deem them to be signs of the power and greatness of the knowing and powerful creator. Prophets and their followers believe that the world is a creation of the beneficent and merciful God and all goodness is from Him and a policy connected to the world is in His hands. The world is not futile and a plaything, on the contrary it is created for a special aim.

They also have a special view and opinion with regard to man and his success. They consider him to be a respectful, exalted and a chosen being, who is a compound of two aspects: a body, which is made of clay and a soul, which is created from the ethereal and celestial world. That is why he is a superior being, everlasting, trustful and trustworthy one of the Lord and who is answerable to Him.

In this view, real success and perfection of man lies in recognition of God, movement towards Him and satisfaction in His pleasure; and since all power and goodness is only from Him, attention to Him leads to all goodness and lofty human values.

The first words of the prophets called to the worship of God and His oneness and negation of every type of polytheism. Prophets considered worship of God and monotheism as the foundations of human values and nobility and forgetting God and carelessness about the remembrance of the Lord as the roots of all evils and attachment to other than God as factors of destruction and misfortune.

Future of man and resurrection in the view of the prophets are perfectly clear, full of hope and nice. Prophets believe that the righteous and believing man will have a bright and comfortable future. He is traveling from this world to the world of the hereafter, which is much more vast and superior to this world and there he would see the final consequences of his deeds.

That is why prophets were having such clear and definite belief with regard to the world, man, success of man and his future; and they had perfect faith in this lofty and true view of theirs.

Foundation of the call of the prophets

Foundation of the call of the prophets was this same world view and they based their religion and code of law (*Shariah*) on it. The first sentence of Prophet Nuh (a) to his people was:

$$\text{اعْبُدُوا اللَّهَ مَا لَكُم مِّنْ إِلَٰهٍ غَيْرُهُ إِنِّي أَخَافُ عَلَيْكُمْ عَذَابَ يَوْمٍ عَظِيمٍ}$$

"...serve Allah, you have no god other than Him; surely I fear for you the chastisement of a grievous day." (7:59)

The first words of Prophet Hud (a) to his people were:

$$\text{اعْبُدُوا اللَّهَ مَا لَكُم مِّنْ إِلَٰهٍ غَيْرُهُ إِنْ أَنتُمْ إِلَّا مُفْتَرُونَ}$$

"...serve Allah, you have no god other than He; you are nothing but forgers (of lies)." (Surah Hud 11:50)

The first statement of Prophet Salih (a) to his people was:

$$\text{اعْبُدُوا اللَّهَ مَا لَكُم مِّنْ إِلَٰهٍ غَيْرُهُ هُوَ أَنشَأَكُم مِّنَ الْأَرْضِ وَاسْتَعْمَرَكُمْ فِيهَا فَاسْتَغْفِرُوهُ ثُمَّ تُوبُوا إِلَيْهِ إِنَّ رَبِّي قَرِيبٌ مُّجِيبٌ}$$

"O my people! serve Allah, you have no god other than He; He brought you into being from the earth, and made you dwell in it, therefore ask forgiveness of Him, then turn to Him; surely my Lord is Nigh, Answering." (11:61)

Prophet Shuaib (a) also, in the beginning of his prophethood, said to the people:

يَٰقَوْمِ ٱعْبُدُوا۟ ٱللَّهَ مَا لَكُم مِّنْ إِلَٰهٍ غَيْرُهُۥ وَلَا تَنقُصُوا۟ ٱلْمِكْيَالَ وَٱلْمِيزَانَ إِنِّىٓ أَرَىٰكُم بِخَيْرٍ وَإِنِّىٓ أَخَافُ عَلَيْكُمْ عَذَابَ يَوْمٍ مُّحِيطٍ ۝ وَيَٰقَوْمِ أَوْفُوا۟ ٱلْمِكْيَالَ وَٱلْمِيزَانَ بِٱلْقِسْطِ وَلَا تَبْخَسُوا۟ ٱلنَّاسَ أَشْيَآءَهُمْ وَلَا تَعْثَوْا۟ فِى ٱلْأَرْضِ مُفْسِدِينَ ۝

"O my people! serve Allah, you have no god other than He, and do not give short measure and weight: surely I see you in prosperity and surely I fear for you the punishment of an all-encompassing day. And, O my people! give full measure and weight fairly, and defraud not men their things, and do not act corruptly in the land, making mischief." (84-85)

Almighty Allah has said with regard to the messengership of Musa (a):

وَلَقَدْ أَرْسَلْنَا مُوسَىٰ بِـَٔايَٰتِنَا وَسُلْطَٰنٍ مُّبِينٍ ۝ إِلَىٰ فِرْعَوْنَ وَمَلَإِيْهِۦ فَٱتَّبَعُوٓا۟ أَمْرَ فِرْعَوْنَ وَمَآ أَمْرُ فِرْعَوْنَ بِرَشِيدٍ ۝ يَقْدُمُ قَوْمَهُۥ يَوْمَ ٱلْقِيَٰمَةِ فَأَوْرَدَهُمُ ٱلنَّارَ وَبِئْسَ ٱلْوِرْدُ ٱلْمَوْرُودُ ۝

"And certainly We sent Musa with Our communications and a clear authority. To Firon and his chiefs, but they followed the bidding of Firon, and Firon's bidding was not right-directing. He shall lead his people on the resurrection day, and bring them down to the fire; and evil the place to which they are brought." (96-98)

In continuation of these verses, He says:

يَوْمَ يَأْتِ لَا تَكَلَّمُ نَفْسٌ إِلَّا بِإِذْنِهِۦ فَمِنْهُمْ شَقِىٌّ وَسَعِيدٌ ۝ فَأَمَّا ٱلَّذِينَ شَقُوا۟ فَفِى ٱلنَّارِ

لَهُمْ فِيهَا زَفِيرٌ وَشَهِيقٌ ۞ خَٰلِدِينَ فِيهَا مَا دَامَتِ ٱلسَّمَٰوَٰتُ وَٱلْأَرْضُ إِلَّا مَا شَآءَ رَبُّكَ إِنَّ رَبَّكَ فَعَّالٌ لِّمَا يُرِيدُ ۞ وَأَمَّا ٱلَّذِينَ سُعِدُوا فَفِى ٱلْجَنَّةِ خَٰلِدِينَ فِيهَا مَا دَامَتِ ٱلسَّمَٰوَٰتُ وَٱلْأَرْضُ إِلَّا مَا شَآءَ رَبُّكَ عَطَآءً غَيْرَ مَجْذُوذٍ ۞

"On the day when it shall come, no soul shall speak except with His permission, then (some) of them shall be unhappy and (others) happy. So as to those who are unhappy, they shall be in the fire; for them shall be sighing and groaning in it: Abiding therein so long as the heavens and the earth endure, except as your Lord please; surely your Lord is the mighty doer of what He intends. And as to those who are made happy, they shall be in the garden, abiding in it as long as the heavens and the earth endure, except as your Lord please; a gift which shall never be cut off." (11:105-108)

If we look carefully, we would see that two basic pillars are present in the call of all the prophets:

1. Worship of One God and 2. Future of man, his success or misfortune. (Resurrection); therefore, faith in these two basics of monotheism and resurrection shape the foundation of the call of the prophets. The prophets, by establishing evidence and proof and by showing miracle, call people to faith in these two basics motivating them to contemplate and ponder on the secrets and mysteries of the world, awaken their God-searching nature, so that they may worship God only. And through their religious view, they may witness the signs of His power in every corner of the world; that they may discover the aim of the creation of man and have faith in the world after death and may be thoughtful about their success or misfortune in future.

First of all, the prophets reformed the beliefs of the people with regard to God and resurrection, as they are the complete basis of all their deeds and behavior. After that they entrusted to them the heavenly program and their code of divine laws. And in this way they called them to goodness and reformation. But the faith, morals and manners of all are according to ones faith and belief. Hence true faith lead to good deeds and puts forth beautiful blossoms. And the result of corrupted and improper belief is nothing, but destruction and injustice. Thus reformation of people requires the reformation of their world view and beliefs. And the same method was employed by the prophets. Faith in God and Judgment Day strengthens the hearts of people so that they may not struggle except on the path Almighty Allah and that they do not accept the obedience of anyone other than Almighty Allah.

Prophets and unity of method and aim

Throughout history thousands of prophets have come from Almighty Allah for the guidance of man; some of them came with a special code of laws and others were missionaries of the religion of the previous prophets. Ultimately, the principle of heavenly religions and program of all the prophets was one and the same. All of them invited man to one and the same aim. Collectively, all the heavenly religions rest on the following three fundamentals:

First: Recognition of one God, who has created the world and faith in Him (monotheism);

Second: Belief in resurrection and the world of the hereafter and the everlasting future of man (resurrection);

Third: Belief in prophets, unity of the way and their way and aims (prophethood);

Prophets called man to accept these basic fundamentals and asked them so that they may adopt the guiding program of religion into their lives and that they should submit to the commands of the wise God. They should base the program of their life only according to the program that religion has chalked for them. All the prophets from Adam to the Messenger of Allah (ṣ) have called man to this same reality. They have named this path that is chosen and liked by God for men as the 'religion of God'. It is only one religion and not more than that.

There is not the smallest difference between the principles and generalities of the call of the prophets and each of them mentioned the previous prophet with respect and honor and followed his methods and message. In the same way, they gave glad tidings of the advent of the coming prophet and informed their followers to have faith in him and accept his call. Almighty Allah has also said in the Holy Quran:

وَإِذْ أَخَذَ ٱللَّهُ مِيثَٰقَ ٱلنَّبِيِّۦنَ لَمَآ ءَاتَيْتُكُم مِّن كِتَٰبٍ وَحِكْمَةٍ ثُمَّ جَآءَكُمْ رَسُولٌ مُّصَدِّقٌ لِّمَا مَعَكُمْ لَتُؤْمِنُنَّ بِهِۦ وَلَتَنصُرُنَّهُۥ ۚ قَالَ ءَأَقْرَرْتُمْ وَأَخَذْتُمْ عَلَىٰ ذَٰلِكُمْ إِصْرِى ۖ قَالُوٓاْ أَقْرَرْنَا ۚ قَالَ فَٱشْهَدُواْ وَأَنَا۠ مَعَكُم مِّنَ ٱلشَّٰهِدِينَ ۝

"And when Allah made a covenant through the prophets: Certainly what I have given you of Book and wisdom- then an apostle comes to you verifying that which is with you, you must believe in him, and you must aid him. He said: Do you affirm and accept My compact in this (matter)? They said: We do affirm. He

said: *Then bear witness, and I (too) am of the bearers of witness with you." (3:81)*

The Holy Quran says thus with regard to faith in prophets and the unity of their way and aim:

$$\text{قُلْ ءَامَنَّا بِٱللَّهِ وَمَآ أُنزِلَ عَلَيْنَا وَمَآ أُنزِلَ عَلَىٰٓ إِبْرَٰهِيمَ وَإِسْمَٰعِيلَ وَإِسْحَٰقَ وَيَعْقُوبَ وَٱلْأَسْبَاطِ وَمَآ أُوتِىَ مُوسَىٰ وَعِيسَىٰ وَٱلنَّبِيُّونَ مِن رَّبِّهِمْ لَا نُفَرِّقُ بَيْنَ أَحَدٍ مِّنْهُمْ وَنَحْنُ لَهُۥ مُسْلِمُونَ ۝ وَمَن يَبْتَغِ غَيْرَ ٱلْإِسْلَٰمِ دِينًا فَلَن يُقْبَلَ مِنْهُ وَهُوَ فِى ٱلْءَاخِرَةِ مِنَ ٱلْخَٰسِرِينَ ۝}$$

"Say: We believe in Allah and what has been revealed to us, and what was revealed to Ibrahim and Ismail and Ishaq and Yaqub and the tribes, and what was given to Musa and Isa and to the prophets from their Lord; we do not make any distinction between any of them, and to Him do we submit. And whoever desires a religion other than Islam, it shall not be accepted from him, and in the hereafter he shall be one of the losers." (3:84-85)

Islam means submission to the command and religion of God. In this meaning, all the prophets were 'Muslims' (those who submit), although terminologically Islam is the last heavenly religion brought by Prophet Muhammad (s) for mankind and Muslim is a follower of this faith.

Prophet Ibrahim (a) in his supplication to Almighty Allah prayed in this way:

$$\text{رَبَّنَا وَٱجْعَلْنَا مُسْلِمَيْنِ لَكَ وَمِن ذُرِّيَّتِنَآ أُمَّةً مُّسْلِمَةً لَّكَ وَأَرِنَا مَنَاسِكَنَا وَتُبْ عَلَيْنَآ إِنَّكَ أَنتَ ٱلتَّوَّابُ ٱلرَّحِيمُ ۝ رَبَّنَا وَٱبْعَثْ فِيهِمْ رَسُولًا مِّنْهُمْ يَتْلُوا۟ عَلَيْهِمْ}$$

ءَايَٰتِكَ وَيُعَلِّمُهُمُ ٱلْكِتَٰبَ وَٱلْحِكْمَةَ وَيُزَكِّيهِمْ إِنَّكَ أَنتَ ٱلْعَزِيزُ ٱلْحَكِيمُ ﴿١٢٩﴾ وَمَن يَرْغَبُ عَن مِّلَّةِ إِبْرَٰهِۦمَ إِلَّا مَن سَفِهَ نَفْسَهُۥ ۚ وَلَقَدِ ٱصْطَفَيْنَٰهُ فِى ٱلدُّنْيَا ۖ وَإِنَّهُۥ فِى ٱلْءَاخِرَةِ لَمِنَ ٱلصَّٰلِحِينَ ﴿١٣٠﴾ إِذْ قَالَ لَهُۥ رَبُّهُۥٓ أَسْلِمْ ۖ قَالَ أَسْلَمْتُ لِرَبِّ ٱلْعَٰلَمِينَ ﴿١٣١﴾ وَوَصَّىٰ بِهَآ إِبْرَٰهِۦمُ بَنِيهِ وَيَعْقُوبُ يَٰبَنِىَّ إِنَّ ٱللَّهَ ٱصْطَفَىٰ لَكُمُ ٱلدِّينَ فَلَا تَمُوتُنَّ إِلَّا وَأَنتُم مُّسْلِمُونَ ﴿١٣٢﴾ أَمْ كُنتُمْ شُهَدَآءَ إِذْ حَضَرَ يَعْقُوبَ ٱلْمَوْتُ إِذْ قَالَ لِبَنِيهِ مَا تَعْبُدُونَ مِنۢ بَعْدِى قَالُوا۟ نَعْبُدُ إِلَٰهَكَ وَإِلَٰهَ ءَابَآئِكَ إِبْرَٰهِۦمَ وَإِسْمَٰعِيلَ وَإِسْحَٰقَ إِلَٰهًا وَٰحِدًا وَنَحْنُ لَهُۥ مُسْلِمُونَ ﴿١٣٣﴾

"Our Lord! and make us both submissive to Thee and (raise) from our offspring a nation submitting to Thee, and show us our ways of devotion and turn to us (mercifully), surely Thou art the Oft-returning (to mercy), the Merciful. Our Lord! and raise up in them an Apostle from among them who shall recite to them Thy communications and teach them the Book and the wisdom, and purify them; surely Thou art the Mighty, the Wise. And who forsakes the religion of Ibrahim but he who makes himself a fool, and most certainly We chose him in this world, and in the hereafter he is most surely among the righteous. When his Lord said to him, Be a Muslim, he said: I submit myself to the Lord of the worlds. And the same did Ibrahim enjoin on his sons and (so did) Yaqub. O my sons! surely Allah has chosen for you (this) faith, therefore die not unless you are Muslims. Nay! were you witnesses when death visited Yaqub, when he said to his sons: What will you serve after me? They said: We will serve your God and the God of your fathers, Ibrahim and Ismail and Ishaq, one God only, and to Him do we submit." (2:128-133)

Two World Views

That is why Almighty Allah has introduced the prophets with one aim, which is the same submission before Allah and those who are opposed to their ways and manners are termed as foolish and ignorant, like in the following verses:

وَرَسُولًا إِلَىٰ بَنِىٓ إِسْرَٰٓءِيلَ أَنِّى قَدْ جِئْتُكُم بِـَٔايَةٍ مِّن رَّبِّكُمْ أَنِّىٓ أَخْلُقُ لَكُم مِّنَ ٱلطِّينِ كَهَيْـَٔةِ ٱلطَّيْرِ فَأَنفُخُ فِيهِ فَيَكُونُ طَيْرًۢا بِإِذْنِ ٱللَّهِ ۖ وَأُبْرِئُ ٱلْأَكْمَهَ وَٱلْأَبْرَصَ وَأُحْىِ ٱلْمَوْتَىٰ بِإِذْنِ ٱللَّهِ ۖ وَأُنَبِّئُكُم بِمَا تَأْكُلُونَ وَمَا تَدَّخِرُونَ فِى بُيُوتِكُمْ ۚ إِنَّ فِى ذَٰلِكَ لَـَٔايَةً لَّكُمْ إِن كُنتُم مُّؤْمِنِينَ ۝ وَمُصَدِّقًا لِّمَا بَيْنَ يَدَىَّ مِنَ ٱلتَّوْرَىٰةِ وَلِأُحِلَّ لَكُم بَعْضَ ٱلَّذِى حُرِّمَ عَلَيْكُمْ ۚ وَجِئْتُكُم بِـَٔايَةٍ مِّن رَّبِّكُمْ فَٱتَّقُوا۟ ٱللَّهَ وَأَطِيعُونِ ۝ إِنَّ ٱللَّهَ رَبِّى وَرَبُّكُمْ فَٱعْبُدُوهُ ۗ هَـٰذَا صِرَٰطٌ مُّسْتَقِيمٌ ۝ فَلَمَّآ أَحَسَّ عِيسَىٰ مِنْهُمُ ٱلْكُفْرَ قَالَ مَنْ أَنصَارِىٓ إِلَى ٱللَّهِ ۖ قَالَ ٱلْحَوَارِيُّونَ نَحْنُ أَنصَارُ ٱللَّهِ ءَامَنَّا بِٱللَّهِ وَٱشْهَدْ بِأَنَّا مُسْلِمُونَ ۝ رَبَّنَآ ءَامَنَّا بِمَآ أَنزَلْتَ وَٱتَّبَعْنَا ٱلرَّسُولَ فَٱكْتُبْنَا مَعَ ٱلشَّـٰهِدِينَ ۝

"And (make him) an apostle to the children of Israel: That I have come to you with a sign from your Lord, that I determine for you out of dust like the form of a bird, then I breathe into it and it becomes a bird with Allah's permission and I heal the blind and the leprous, and bring the dead to life with Allah's permission and I inform you of what you should eat and what you should store in your houses; most surely there is a sign in this for you, if you are believers. And a verifier of that which is before me of the Taurat and that I may allow you part of that which has been forbidden you, and I have come to you with a sign from your Lord therefore be careful of (your duty to)

Allah and obey me. Surely Allah is my Lord and your Lord, therefore serve Him; this is the right path. But when Isa perceived unbelief on their part, he said: Who will be my helpers in Allah's way? The disciples said: We are helpers (in the way) of Allah: We believe in Allah and bear witness that we are submitting ones. Our Lord! we believe in what Thou hast revealed and we follow the apostle, so write us down with those who bear witness." (3:49-53)

All divine prophets like teachers of the same school, are sent one after another to call human beings to submission to religion of God and that by their guidance, they may lead man to the path of perfection, which is the same straight path. Religion and aim of the prophets was common and all of them made efforts to gain the satisfaction of Almighty Allah and His proximity. There was no difference between the heavenly religions of the prophets, except in secondary laws of religions. And that too was due to difference in conditions and circumstances as also the capacities of people. Circumstances, levels of understanding and capabilities of people were not same during all ages, therefore the prophets spoke to the people in accordance to the level of their understanding and gradually bestowed to them perfection and maturity in understanding and awareness in accepting the concepts of religion till prophethood reached to the last of the prophets, Prophet Muhammad Mustafa (ṣ). He was sent for the guidance of people with such detailed and specific principles of faith that no prophet before him had come with such details. He came with a comprehensive set of laws and greatness of religion cognition that his religion included all the modes of contemplation, reasoning and research. And the religion that he brought was the last and the most detailed code of law and faith that Almighty Allah has ever sent for humanity. Almighty Allah has said with regard to the comprehensiveness of the religion of Islam as compared to the previous faith as follows:

شَرَعَ لَكُم مِّنَ ٱلدِّينِ مَا وَصَّىٰ بِهِۦ نُوحًا وَٱلَّذِىٓ أَوْحَيْنَآ إِلَيْكَ وَمَا وَصَّيْنَا بِهِۦٓ إِبْرَٰهِيمَ وَمُوسَىٰ وَعِيسَىٰٓ أَنْ أَقِيمُوا۟ ٱلدِّينَ وَلَا تَتَفَرَّقُوا۟ فِيهِ كَبُرَ عَلَى ٱلْمُشْرِكِينَ مَا تَدْعُوهُمْ إِلَيْهِ ٱللَّهُ يَجْتَبِىٓ إِلَيْهِ مَن يَشَآءُ وَيَهْدِىٓ إِلَيْهِ مَن يُنِيبُ ۝

"He has made plain to you of the religion what He enjoined upon Nuh and that which We have revealed to you and that which We enjoined upon Ibrahim and Musa and Isa that keep to obedience and be not divided therein; hard to the unbelievers is that which you call them to; Allah chooses for Himself whom He pleases, and guides to Himself him who turns (to Him), frequently." (42:13)

PERSEVERANCE OF THE PROPHETS

Faith in God and the world of the hereafter is infused into the depths of the souls of the prophets and has reached to the level of certainty and spiritual realization. They had contacts with the unseen world and they had not the slightest doubt about their office. They had trust in the unlimited power of God and did not fear any other force. They were determined in fulfilling their celestial responsibilities and did not fear the shortage of strength. Multitude of difficulties and obstruction of the enemies did not in any way disrupt their strong determination and they made efforts to solve the problems of the society with steadfastness and resolve. The same decisiveness and determination can be considered as the most important factor of their success. Study of the life of the prophets and their struggle is extremely remarkable and edifying. Below we shall mention some of them in brief:

Perseverance of Prophet Ibrahim (a)

This great divine prophet rose up all alone against polytheism and idol worship and single-handed confronted Nimrod's regime, which supported idols and idol worship and he was not cowed down by Nimrod's power; he said with full determination:

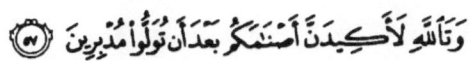

"And, by Allah! I will certainly do something against your idols after you go away, turning back." (21:57)

He staged an uprising all alone in order to destroy the idols. One day when the idol worshippers were out of town, Ibrahim (a) entered a huge temple and broke down all the idols. When the tyrannical court condemned him to be thrown into the inferno for his crime of destroying the idols, he did not display slightest weakness and regret and remained firm in defense of his beliefs. So much so that when he was tossed by the catapult into the middle of the inferno, he showed no weakness from his side and did not ask for the help of anyone other than Almighty Allah till by the will of Allah the fire became cool and safe for him.

Steadfastness of Ibrahim (a) in confrontation with idol worship and establishment of monotheism was to such an extent that the Holy Quran has mentioned him to be a single nation:

إِنَّ إِبْرَٰهِيمَ كَانَ أُمَّةً قَانِتًا لِّلَّهِ حَنِيفًا وَلَمْ يَكُ مِنَ ٱلْمُشْرِكِينَ ﴿١٢٠﴾

"Surely Ibrahim was an exemplar, obedient to Allah, upright, and he was not of the polytheists." (16:120)

Perseverance of Prophet Musa (a)

His Eminence, Musa (a) was also sent with messengership and was appointed by Almighty Allah to approach the court of the tyrant Firon to convey His message and to save the oppressed community of Bani Israel from him. He finally went to the huge palace of Firon dressed only in simple clothes, carrying a staff and accompanied by none but his brother, Harun. He was in no way cowed down by the magnificence of the grand palace or the power of the tyrannical Firon; and with perfect confidence said:

$$\text{وَقَالَ مُوسَىٰ يَٰفِرْعَوْنُ إِنِّى رَسُولٌ مِّن رَّبِّ ٱلْعَٰلَمِينَ ۝ حَقِيقٌ عَلَىٰٓ أَن لَّآ أَقُولَ عَلَى ٱللَّهِ إِلَّا ٱلْحَقَّ قَدْ جِئْتُكُم بِبَيِّنَةٍ مِّن رَّبِّكُمْ فَأَرْسِلْ مَعِىَ بَنِىٓ إِسْرَٰٓءِيلَ ۝}$$

"And Musa said: O Firon! surely I am an apostle from the Lord of the worlds: (I am) worthy of not saying anything about Allah except the truth: I have come to you indeed with clear proof from your Lord, therefore send with me the children of Israel." (7:104-105)

Prophet Musa (a) confronted the tyrant Firon for years in order to call people to monotheism and to save Bani Israel and displayed patience and steadfastness in front of all kinds of oppressions of the people of Firon. And even though surrounded by hardships, he encouraged Bani Israel to observe patience and perseverance and he said:

$$\text{قَالَ مُوسَىٰ لِقَوْمِهِ ٱسْتَعِينُوا۟ بِٱللَّهِ وَٱصْبِرُوٓا۟ إِنَّ ٱلْأَرْضَ لِلَّهِ يُورِثُهَا مَن يَشَآءُ مِنْ عِبَادِهِ وَٱلْعَٰقِبَةُ لِلْمُتَّقِينَ ۝}$$

"Musa said to his people: Ask help from Allah and be patient; surely the land is Allah's; He causes such of His servants to inherit it as He pleases, and the end is for those who guard (against evil)." (7:128)

The people of Musa (a), whose patience was depleted, said:

$$\text{قَالُوٓا۟ أُوذِينَا مِن قَبْلِ أَن تَأْتِيَنَا وَمِنۢ بَعْدِ مَا جِئْتَنَا}$$

"They said: We have been persecuted before you came to us and since you have come to us." (7:129)

In order to encourage and motivate them, Prophet Musa (a) said:

$$قَالَ عَسَىٰ رَبُّكُمْ أَن يُهْلِكَ عَدُوَّكُمْ وَيَسْتَخْلِفَكُمْ فِى ٱلْأَرْضِ فَيَنظُرَ كَيْفَ تَعْمَلُونَ ۝$$

"He said: It may be that your Lord will destroy your enemy and make you rulers in the land; then He will see how you act." (7:129)

In the final days of his important and risky office, Prophet Musa (a) displayed such perseverance that in the end he was successful and destroyed Firon and his accursed tyranny and saved Bani Israel from the disgrace of slavery, oppression, torture and killings at the hands of the Egyptians.

Perseverance of Prophet Muhammad (ṣ)

Muhammad (ṣ) rose up all alone against polytheism and idol worship and with deep-rooted determination and decisive will, struggled to achieve his lofty aim and was determined in front of different kinds of difficulties. Throughout the period of 23 years of his prophethood, when he was faced with extremely troublesome hardships, he did not display even the least weakness and doubt. He was bestowed the office of prophethood by Almighty Allah so that he may be absolutely steadfastness in achieving his final aim. In the Holy Quran, Almighty Allah says:

$$فَٱسْتَقِمْ كَمَا أُمِرْتَ وَمَن تَابَ مَعَكَ وَلَا تَطْغَوْا إِنَّهُ بِمَا تَعْمَلُونَ بَصِيرٌ ۝$$

"Continue then in the right way as you are commanded, as also he who has turned (to Allah) with you, and be not inordinate (O men!), surely He sees what you do." (11:112)

The Prophet of Islam, throughout the period of his messengership and even at the beginning of his call, explained his message clearly and decisively and did have any fear of the multitude of the enemies. At the time, the following verse was revealed:

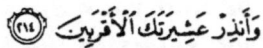

"And warn your nearest relations," (26:214)

...he was given the charge to make his call open, he ordered Ali Ibn Abi Talib (a): Prepare some food and invite the relatives, so that I may call them to Islam. Ali (a), according to the order of the Holy Prophet (ṣ), prepared food and invited approximately forty of their relatives for dinner. After the dinner, the Prophet wanted to address the guests, but Abu Lahab interrupted and prevented him from it till the time all the guests dispersed. Ali Ibn Abi Talib (a) said: I repeated the procedure under the orders of the Messenger of Allah (ṣ) and again he was prevented from addressing the audience. I again organized a dinner on the third day and after that the Holy Prophet (ṣ) addressed his relatives:

"O sons of Abdul Muttalib, by Allah, I don't know of any young man who was appointed to his people better than me. I have brought the well being of the world and the hereafter for you. Allah has commanded me to call you to Him.

Thus, who will help me in this matter, so that he may be my successor and legatee?" Ali (a) has described their reaction thus: All of them turned away and did not accept.

Thus, I, who was the youngest of all, and the sharpest and most sensitive of them, said: I will be your helper and vicegerent, O Messenger of Allah (ṣ). The Holy Prophet (ṣ) tapped my back and said: He is my brother, my successor and my vicegerent among you. Listen to him and obey him. After that people arose laughing and said to Abu Talib, "He is commanding you to listen to your son and to obey him."[1]

Polytheist employed every means to obstruct the mission of the Prophet, but he also observed steadfastness and perseverance. One day Quraish leaders came to Abu Talib, uncle of Prophet and said:

"O Abu Talib, you are senior in age and nobility and before this we had asked you to restrain your nephew, but you have not done that. By Allah, we cannot remain patient on the fact that someone should talk ill of our gods and ancestors and that he should consider our dream to be foolishness; but that you prevent him from us or we would confront him and you till one of us is killed." As mentioned before, they said this and went away from there.

Abu Talib was troubled by the aloofness of the people and their enmity. Their non-acceptance of Islam and leaving the Prophet was also unbearable for him. So he sent a messenger to the Prophet to apprise him of the situation and tell him: Ensure yours as well as my well being. And do not impose upon that which I cannot bear. The Holy Prophet (ṣ) thought something has befallen his uncle and that he was leaving him to his own devices. Therefore the Messenger of Allah (ṣ) said:

---

[1] *Al-Kamil fit Tarikh*, Vol. 1, Pg. 487-488

O uncle, if they place the sun in my right hand and the moon in the left, I will never give up this matter, except that I make it evident or I die.[1]

The Prophet of Islam (ṣ) faced a world full of polytheism and infidelity and in the stages of his propagation, he had to bear hundreds of problems; the people troubled him time and again and subjected his few followers to different types of troubles and tortures. He and his followers were confined in the defile of Abu Talib and subjected to economic embargo. His life was always in danger and many a times they planned to eliminate him and gave him other troubles. But he continued to perform the duties of his office with absolute determination and resolve till finally he came out successful over his enemies and hoisted the flag of monotheism over the world. Through this medium, he taught the Muslims, worshippers of God and reformers, a lesson in patience and steadfastness.

---

[1] *Al-Kamil fit Tarikh*, Vol. 1, Pg. 488-489

PART TWO
PROPHET OF ISLAM
SPECIAL PROPHETHOOD

EVIDENCES OF THE PROPHETHOOD OF MUHAMMAD

For recognition of the true divine prophets – like Muhammad (ṣ) – we can use the following methods:

1. Study and conduct a detailed research into the manners and morals, and the life of the claimant of prophethood.

2. Study and contemplate on the set of principles of belief, laws, rules and regulations, which are introduced as religion.

3. Check the news and glad tidings that are received from the preceding divine prophets about him.

4. Take into consideration his performance of extraordinary acts and miracle, which other human beings cannot accomplish.

By studying the history of the early period of Islam, we come to know that the Muslims of that time were not same in acceptance of Islam; that all of them did not demand miracles from the prophet or some of them did not bring faith even after witnessing those miracles. On the contrary, getting faith and satisfaction in the prophethood of the Prophet and the veracity of his claim was generally through other means. At this point, we shall mention some of those means:

First method

By studying the early history of Islam, it is known that some persons were influenced by the extraordinary personality, good manners, nice character, trustworthiness, truthfulness and honesty of Muhammad (s) and his good antecedents, and in this way they were assured about the veracity of the claim of his prophethood and they brought faith on him.

Muhammad (s), before being vested with the office of prophethood and even during his childhood possessed a remarkable personality and became famed for his benevolence, honesty, helping the deprived and weak, truthfulness and right behavior and he did not have even the slightest blemish on his past. Some people accepted his claim of prophethood and they accepted faith in this manner.

Lady Khadija (a) can be considered to be the chief of such persons as she was the first of those who accepted his invitation and embraced Islam. She knew Prophet Muhammad (s) and his spiritual qualities and perfections better than others, and was most cognizant of him in ranks of truth and piety. That is why she accepted faith much before others. Therefore she considered these personal qualities to be the evidence of the veracity of his claim, which persuaded her to follow his messengership.

It is mentioned in history that after Muhammad (ṣ) saw Jibraeel (a) in the cave of Hira, and received the first revelation, he hurried home and narrated the incident to his wife, Lady Khadija (a).

He says: I came to Khadija and said: "I am fearful for my life." Then he narrated the incident of seeing Jibraeel and his message. Khadija replied, "Glad tiding be to you by Allah, He has not degraded you in any way. By Allah, you are nice to your kin, truthful and honest, you share the difficulties of others, are hospitable and help others in the problems of the world."[1]

Sometimes the Messenger of Allah (ṣ) took this matter as the evidence of his messengership and asked people to accept his prophethood.

Bulazari writes: When the verse of:

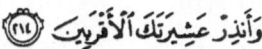

"And warn your nearest relations," (26:214)

...was revealed on Prophet Muhammad (ṣ), he climbed Mount Safa and called the Quraish in a loud voice and Quraish heard him and remarked: Muhammad is on Mount Safa and he is calling you. All of them came to him and asked: O Muhammad, why have you summoned us? He replied: "Would you believe me if I tell you that enemy riders have come behind this mountain and are about to launch an attack on you?" Yes, they said, "We would definitely believe you, because we have never seen you lying. He said: "So I warn you of the chastisement of Judgment Day. O sons of Abdul

---

[1] *Al-Kamil fit Tarikh*, Vol. 1, Pg. 478

Muttalib, O sons of Abd Manaf, O sons of Zahra! (and he mentioned the Quraish tribes). Allah has commanded me to call my near relatives to Islam. I do not consider anything more beneficial for your world and hereafter except that you say: There is no god, except Allah."[1]

Ali Ibn Abi Talib (a) also accepted Islam in this way. He was the first among men that at the beginning of the Prophet's mission accepted his call and embraced faith as a result of recognition and assurance with regard to him.

Abu Bakr also became a Muslim in this manner. Abul Fida has narrated from Ibn Ishaq that Abu Bakr used to cultivate the company of the Prophet before his being vested by the office of prophethood and was so much aware of his truthfulness, trustworthiness and honesty that he knew him to be immune from attributing falsehood to people, far be it from him that he should attribute falsehood to Almighty God.[2]

Most Muslims in the early period of Islam embraced faith in this way since they were satisfied with the truthfulness and honesty of the Prophet and they knew that he never resorted to lying; therefore they believed his claim of prophethood and messengership with perfect certainty and embraced faith.

In the near future, we would discuss about the prominent and magnetic personality of the Messenger of Allah (ṣ) and his good manners and praiseworthy qualities.

---

[1] *Ansabul Ashraf*, Vol. 1, Pg. 120
[2] Abul Fida, *Seerat Nabuwwa*, Vol. 1, Pg. 433

Second method

Recognizing the veracity of a religion and to be sure that it is heavenly, and verification of the message brought by it, can be undertaken through study and investigation in the text of its belief and ethical laws. If the beliefs proposed by it possess qualities like: compatibility with reason, and that it is opposed to superstitions, it is comprehensive and reliever of the social and moral difficulties of people, it calls people to good morals and character and restrains them from social and moral corruption, it would be known that this religion is true and that it is heavenly, and that it has really come from Almighty God and the true prophets of God.

But if the beliefs of that religion are dubious and invalid and its laws are weak and baseless, and they cannot solve social and moral problems, it would be known that its claimant is a liar and his religion is futile and invalid.

Some Muslims in the early period of Islam embraced faith in this same way. After study and contemplation about the beliefs and laws of Islam, they concluded that the proposal and compilation of such lofty and hundred percent correct and perfect beliefs could not be possible through an uneducated person, and also that they should be announced in a backward society mired in idol worship and moral decadence of the Arabian Peninsula; on the contrary they should be from Almighty Allah. At this point we shall mention some examples of this:

Amr ibn Ambasa says: In the early period of Islam, I came to the Messenger of Allah (s) at a time when he lived in fear of his life. I asked: Who are you? He replied: I am a messenger. I asked: Whose messenger? He replied: Messenger of Allah.

I asked: Has God really sent you? He replied: Yes. I asked: What has He sent you for? He said: That you should worship Him alone and do not associate anyone with Him. That you should break the idols and have good relations with your kin. I asked: He has sent you with a nice purpose...Amr said: I embraced Islam on listening to this.[1]

Abul Fida writes about conversion of Khalid ibn Saeed: Khalid met the Messenger of Allah (ṣ) and asked: To what do you call us? He replied: Faith in One God, Prophethood of Muhammad and keeping aloof from worship of stones that neither hear nor cause any harm, they neither see nor cause any benefit, and neither can they differentiate between their worshippers from others.

On this point, Khalid said: I testify that there is no god, except Allah and that Muhammad is the messenger of Allah. Thus the Messenger of Allah (ṣ) was pleased with his acceptance of faith.[2]

The exchange that took place between the emigrant Muslims and King Negus of Abyssinia also supports this contention.

Ibn Athir has narrated the story of emigration of Muslims in detail, which in brief was as follows:

In the fifth year of migration (*Hijra*), some Muslims who were fed up to be under the yoke of the torture of the enemies of Islam, were compelled to migrate to Abyssinia in order to save their lives and religion. But after sometime Quraish sent two persons in pursuit of the

---

[1] Abul Fida, *Seerat Nabuwwa*, Vol. 1, Pg. 442

[2] Abul Fida, *Seerat Nabuwwa*, Vol. 1, Pg. 445

migrants and they carried with them a lot of gift for the royals of Abyssinia to persuade them to send back the Muslim migrants. So they came to King Negus in Abyssinia and narrated the purpose of their visit. The King summoned the Muslims in asylum and asked: What religion is this, that you have abandoned the faith of your ancestors and not even joined our religion or any other existing faith?

Ja'far ibn Abu Talib – the representative of the people – in reply said: During the period of Ignorance, we worshipped the idols, consumed carrion flesh and committed evil deeds; we broke off relations with our kin and misbehaved with our neighbors, our powerful ones trespassed the rights of our weak till the time, Almighty Allah sent a prophet for us, about whose genealogy we were cognizant and about whose veracity and honesty we were satisfied. He called us to monotheism and negation of polytheism and to give up idol worship; he called us to truthfulness, restoration of trusts and maintaining relations with kin and doing a good turn to the neighbors and to keep away from sins like murder. He restrained us from committing evil acts, false testimony and misappropriation of the property of orphans. He commanded us to pray and keep fasts. Ja'far also mentioned a number of other Islamic rules and regulations. After that he said:

We brought faith on the Prophet of Islam and testified to his call; we considered as unlawful, that which he deemed unlawful and considered as lawful, that which he deemed lawful; therefore we had to bear the oppression and excesses of our friends; they subjected us to severe torture and chastisement so that we may give up our faith and revert to idol worship. Since they gained domination on us we came under the yoke of their oppression; they prevented us from fulfilling our religious duties and we had to migrate to your country and we hope that we will not have to face any injustice here.

King Negus said: Have you anything revealed to him from God? Ja'far replied: Yes, and then he recited some verses of Surah Maryam. The King and his bishops present in the court at that time wept on hearing those verses. Negus said: These statements and that which was revealed on Isa are from an illuminated source. You are free in our country; you may go anywhere you like and by God, I will never hand over you to them.[1]

That is why the manner of study and research in the beliefs and laws of religion can be introduced as a means of recognizing true religions. A large number of people at the beginning of Islam and after that embraced Islam in this way, in this time also there are some seekers of truth who accept Islam in this manner.

At the conclusion of this point, we consider it necessary that although a large number of Muslims in the early period of Islam and after that were satisfied with the rightfulness of the claim of the Prophet and accepted Islam because of it, their certainty is evident proof; but it is possible that for others this method may not be convincing and satisfactory. Therefore it cannot be used as an argument with others. Hence these can be introduced as the evidences of truthfulness and not as absolute argumentations and which can be used in debates.

---

[1] *Al-Kamil fit Tarikh*, Vol. 2, Pg. 79

Prophet of Islam and glad tidings about him

The third method of verifying the claim of prophethood is through the prophecies of the previous prophets which mention his imminent advent. This method can used even in the case of the prophethood of Prophet Muhammad (ṣ). For example, the Holy Quran has mentioned the glad tidings of the prophets with regard to the messengership of Prophet Muhammad (ṣ) and it considers them as undeniable proofs; like the following verses:

وَلَمَّا جَاءَهُمْ كِتَابٌ مِنْ عِنْدِ اللَّهِ مُصَدِّقٌ لِمَا مَعَهُمْ وَكَانُوا مِنْ قَبْلُ يَسْتَفْتِحُونَ عَلَى الَّذِينَ كَفَرُوا فَلَمَّا جَاءَهُمْ مَا عَرَفُوا كَفَرُوا بِهِ فَلَعْنَةُ اللَّهِ عَلَى الْكَافِرِينَ ﴿٨٩﴾

"And when there came to them a Book from Allah verifying that which they have, and aforetime they used to pray for victory against those who disbelieve, but when there came to them (Prophet) that which they did not recognize, they disbelieved in him; so Allah's curse is on the unbelievers." (2:89)

الَّذِينَ آتَيْنَاهُمُ الْكِتَابَ يَعْرِفُونَهُ كَمَا يَعْرِفُونَ أَبْنَاءَهُمْ وَإِنَّ فَرِيقًا مِنْهُمْ لَيَكْتُمُونَ الْحَقَّ وَهُمْ يَعْلَمُونَ ﴿١٤٦﴾

"Those whom We have given the Book recognize him as they recognize their sons, and a party of them most surely conceal the truth while they know (it)." (2:146)

الَّذِينَ يَتَّبِعُونَ الرَّسُولَ النَّبِيَّ الْأُمِّيَّ الَّذِي يَجِدُونَهُ مَكْتُوبًا عِنْدَهُمْ فِي التَّوْرَاةِ وَالْإِنْجِيلِ يَأْمُرُهُمْ بِالْمَعْرُوفِ وَيَنْهَاهُمْ عَنِ الْمُنْكَرِ وَيُحِلُّ لَهُمُ الطَّيِّبَاتِ وَيُحَرِّمُ عَلَيْهِمُ الْخَبَائِثَ وَيَضَعُ عَنْهُمْ إِصْرَهُمْ وَالْأَغْلَالَ الَّتِي كَانَتْ عَلَيْهِمْ فَالَّذِينَ آمَنُوا بِهِ وَعَزَّرُوهُ وَنَصَرُوهُ وَاتَّبَعُوا النُّورَ الَّذِي أُنْزِلَ مَعَهُ أُولَٰئِكَ هُمُ الْمُفْلِحُونَ ﴿١٥٧﴾

"Those who follow the Apostle-Prophet, the unlettered, whom they find written down with them in the Taurat and the Injeel (who) enjoins them good and forbids them evil, and makes lawful to them the good things and makes unlawful to them impure things, and removes from them their burden and the shackles which were upon them; so (as for) those who believe in him and honor him and help him, and follow the light which has been sent down with him, these it is that are the successful." (7:157)

وَإِذْ قَالَ عِيسَى ابْنُ مَرْيَمَ يَٰبَنِىٓ إِسْرَٰٓءِيلَ إِنِّى رَسُولُ ٱللَّهِ إِلَيْكُم مُّصَدِّقًا لِّمَا بَيْنَ يَدَىَّ مِنَ ٱلتَّوْرَىٰةِ وَمُبَشِّرًۢا بِرَسُولٍ يَأْتِى مِنۢ بَعْدِى ٱسْمُهُۥٓ أَحْمَدُ ۖ فَلَمَّا جَآءَهُم بِٱلْبَيِّنَٰتِ قَالُوا۟ هَٰذَا سِحْرٌ مُّبِينٌ ۝٦

"And when Isa son of Maryam said: O children of Israel! surely I am the apostle of Allah to you, verifying that which is before me of the Taurat and giving the good news of an Apostle who will come after me, his name being Ahmad, but when he came to them with clear arguments they said: This is clear magic." (61:6)

It can be concluded from the above verses that during the time of the office of the Messenger of Allah (ṣ) and the revelation of Quran, Jews and Christians, residing in the Arabian Peninsula were in anticipation of the advent of the prophet who would be sent in that land and who would support the belief of God worship and monotheism and help the believers and heavenly religions. Jews and Christians were aware of the distinguishing qualities of that promised prophet and they recognized him just as they recognized their sons. So much so that they also knew that his name would be Ahmad.

It is known that Prophets Isa and Musa (a) and other divine prophets informed about the advent of that prophet and also mentioned his particular qualities; they even stated his name and signs, which are all mentioned in the present Taurat and Injeel. Jews and Christians were having such profound faith in the coming of that prophet that when faced by the oppression of polytheists and not having strength enough to defend themselves they used to warn the idolaters that very soon the promised prophet is to appear who would come to help them.

Ibn Hisham writes: Asim Ibn Umar ibn Qatada has narrated from the men of his tribe that they said: By the favor and guidance of God, Hammad invited us to Islam. We were polytheists and sometimes there were fights between us and some Jews who possessed knowledge that we did not have and they used to warn us: The time for the advent of the promised prophet is near; when he appears we would with him slay you all like the Aad and Iram people. We always heard these threats from them.

Thus when Prophet Muhammad (ṣ) was vested with the office of prophethood, we accepted his call and recognized him to be the same prophet about whom the Jews used to warn us. Thus we took precedence over the Jews and embraced faith; but they remained firm on their denial. Thus verses of Surah Baqarah were revealed about us and them.[1]

Bulazari writes: Safiya, daughter of Abdul Muttalib said to Abu Lahab: Brother is it proper for you to abandon your nephew and his Islam? By Allah, scholars had

---

[1] *Seerat Ibne Hisham*, Vol. 1, Pg. 225

always prophesied that prophethood would appear from the loins of Abdul Muttalib and Muhammad is that same promised prophet.[1]

In books of history also the names of a large number of scholars of the People of the Book and other soothsayers are mentioned who before the advent of the Prophet of Islam were in anticipation of him and they had also informed others about it. Below we shall mention some of them by way of examples:

The Holy Prophet Muhammad (ṣ) during childhood traveled to Syria with his uncle, Abu Talib; on the way he reached a monastery of Bahira who invited the caravan for dinner after he saw extraordinary signs and after he had posed some queries to Abu Talib. Then he told Abu Talib in private: Take your nephew back to your homeland and protect him from Jews; by Allah, if they see and recognize him, they would eliminate him. Know that your nephew would reach a position of greatness.[2]

There was a monk by the name of Aisa who lived in the Dharan province. He was in possession of extensive knowledge and he came to Mecca once a year and interacted with the people there. On one of his visits, he said: O Meccans, very soon a child would be born among you to whom would submit all the Arabs and non-Arabs; the time of his advent is near; and one who lives till that time and embraces faith has in fact fulfilled his desires and one who opposes him has made a mistake. By God, I am awaiting for him.[3]

---

[1] *Ansabul Ashraf*, Vol. 1, Pg. 119
[2] Abul Fida, *Seerat Nabuwwa*, Vol. 1, Pg. 243-245
[3] Abul Fida, *Seerat Nabuwwa*, Vol. 1, Pg. 222

Muhammad ibn Salma says: There was a Jew named Yusha in Bani Ashal. During childhood I heard that he said: Time has approached for the advent of a prophet from this Holy house (Kaaba); one who lives till his time should testify in his favor. Thus, I was alive till the time of the advent of the Prophet of Islam and I embraced faith at his hands; but that Jew, due to jealousy, refused to accept Islam.[1]

Asim ibn Umar says: An elderly man from Bani Quraiza asked me: Do you know the reason why Thalaba ibn Saya, Usaid ibn Saya, Asad ibn Ubaid and some others from Bani Hilal embrace Islam? I replied: No. He said: Some years before Islam a Jew named Ibn Hayyaban came to us in Syria and settled down there. By Allah, I had not seen anyone better than him. He lived with us for a period of time. When he realized that he was about to pass away, he said: O Jews do you know why I settled down here? We replied in the negative. He said: It was so because I was in anticipation of a prophet and the time of his advent is near. And that he would migrate to this town. I was hopeful that he would appear and that I would accept his message. Time is near for the advent of that prophet, others should not precede you in accepting his faith as he would even take up arms against his opponents.

When the Prophet of Islam was vested with the office of prophethood and he besieged Bani Quraiza, these young men said: O Bani Quraiza, by God it is the same prophet about whom Ibn Hayyaban had informed. Bani Quraiza retorted: It is not so. They said: By God, he is the same,

---

[1] Abul Fida, *Seerat Nabuwwa*, Vol. 1, Pg. 294

because he is having those same qualities and signs. Thus they embraced Islam and in this way they made their lives and properties safe.[1]

In some events connected with the past of Salman Farsi and his conversion, it is mentioned that he said: I set out to meet a very senior monk who resided in the vicinity of Jerusalem. He was an extremely elderly man and was accorded respect by one and all. On the way he looked at me and said: I am having a God, and Judgment Day, Paradise, Hell and accounting is before it all. After some good advices he said: O Salman, Almighty Allah will soon send a prophet named Ahmad. He would appear in the land of Mecca. He would accept gifts but not alms. He will be having the seal of prophethood between his shoulders. His time is near, but since I am extremely aged, I don't think I would be able to live till that time. If you live till that time, you must verify him and accept the religion offered by him. Salman said: Even though he may urge me to give up your faith? He replied: Yes, because the truth is with him and his leadership is approved by the Almighty God.[2]

Amir ibn Rabia says: I heard from Zaid ibn Amr ibn Nufayl that he said: I am in anticipation of a prophet from the descendants of Ismail and Abdul Muttalib. I don't think I would life till his time. But I have faith in him and I testify that he is the prophet of God.[3]

---

[1] Abul Fida, *Seerat Nabuwwa*, Vol. 1, Pg. 294
[2] Abul Fida, *Seerat Nabuwwa*, Vol. 1, Pg. 306
[3] Abul Fida, *Seerat Nabuwwa*, Vol. 1, Pg. 159

When Khadija narrated to Waraqa ibn Naufal, a Christian scholar what her slave had seen from The Holy Prophet Muhammad (s) during the journey to Syria or that which he heard from the monk, he told her: If what you say is true, Muhammad is the prophet of this nation. I know that there is a prophet for this nation and I am in anticipation of him.[1]

Although we don't claim that all the prophecies with regard to him are correct. On the contrary, some may even have been interpolated, but from the above mentioned verses and some other prophecies we can conclude that during the time of the vesting of the office of prophethood of the Prophet of Islam and before that prophecies were well known among the people and most people, especially, the People of the Book were awaiting for a prophet, who was about to appear in the Arabian Peninsula and they were also aware of some of his signs.

It is possible that these prophecies spread among the people in two ways: One is from the sayings of the scholars of religion, which continued to go on changing from one language to another and in this way they gained currency among the people and were also recorded in their books occasionally and finally concluded from the statements of previous prophets. The second way is through quoting the heavenly books like: Taurat, Injeel, Zabur etc.

It is concluded from verse 157 of Surah Araaf that some signs of the Prophet of Islam were present in Taurat and Injeel and the Jews and Christians have informed about them. Despite the fact that this verse was heard by all of

---

[1] Abul Fida, *Seerat Nabuwwa*, Vol. 1, Pg. 267

them, they could not refute it in any way. On the contrary, some of them embraced Islam in the same way, some examples of which are mentioned.

Anyway, it is regrettable that most Jews and Christians refused to accept Islam and justified their action on the pretext that the Prophet of Islam should be from Bani Israel, while the fact is that Muhammad is not from Bani Israel. Their scholars played an important role in this regard and in every possible way they tried to restrain the people from accepting Islam. Severe religious prejudices and love of wealth and position did not allow them to accept the truth.

Study of the different prophecies and deep research into Taurat and Injeel, comparison of different versions of the Bible and selection of the correct Bible; proving interpolation in these two books as was claimed needs a long discussion and a separate book, which is not possible at present; therefore we advise to those who are interested to refer to books of prophecies.

Prophet of Islam and Miracle

The fourth method of recognizing heavenly prophets is the display of miracles on their part. That is they perform extraordinary acts which ordinary human beings are not able to accomplish and which are not achieved through the normal process of causes and effects. Since the prophets claimed to have connection with the Lord of the worlds and that they were having knowledge about His message, they were bound to have a proof and miracle as no one other than Almighty Allah can facilitate such a thing.

All the prophets possessed miracles. The Prophet of Islam (s) had accepted the true miracles with regard to the previous prophets. Numerous miracles of the past prophets are mentioned in the Holy Quran. Therefore, it is necessary that he himself should possess a miracle, since it is not right for him to narrate the miracles of the past prophets without himself being able to display them and say: The past prophets possessed miracles to prove their prophethood, but I don't have any miracle, accept my call without miracles.

Hence, the Prophet of Islam (s) also possessed miracles, which are mentioned in books of history.

Bulazari writes: Waraqa said to The Holy Prophet Muhammad (s): No prophet was vested with the office of prophethood except that he had some special signs; thus what is *your* sign? The Messenger of Allah (s) called the tree to move and it split the earth and came towards him. Waraqa said: I testify to your prophethood and if you command me to fight in a holy war on your side, I would accept the proposal and render you all the help that I can.[1]

Imam Ali (a) said: I was with him when a party of the Quraish came to him and said, "O Muhammad, you have made a big claim which none of your fore-fathers or those of your family have made. We ask you one thing; if you give us an answer to it and show it to us, we will believe that you are a prophet and a messenger, but if you cannot do it, we will know that you are a sorcerer and a liar."

---

[1] *Ansabul Ashraf*, Vol. 1, Pg. 106

The Messenger of Allah said: "What do you ask for?" They said: "Ask this tree to move for us, even with its roots, and stop before you." The Prophet said, "Verily, Allah has power over everything. If Allah does it for you, will you then believe and stand witness to the truth?" They said "Yes." Then he said, "I shall show you whatever you want, but I know that you won't bend towards virtue, and there are among you those who will be thrown into the pit, and those who will form parties (against me)." Then the Holy Prophet said: "O tree, if you do believe in Allah and Judgment Day, and know that I am the Prophet of Allah, come up with your roots and stand before me with the permission of Allah." By Him who deputed the Prophet with truth, the tree did remove itself with its root and came with a great humming sound and a flapping like the flapping of the wings of birds, till it stopped before the Messenger of Allah while some of its twigs came down onto my shoulders, and I was on the right side of the Holy Prophet.

When the people saw this, they said by way of pride and vanity. "Now you order half of it to come to you and the other half of it remain (in its place)." The Holy Prophet ordered the tree to do the same. Then half of the tree advanced towards him in an amazing manner and with greater humming. It was about to touch the Prophet of Allah. Then they said, disbelieving and revolting, "Ask this half to get back to its other half and be as it was." The Prophet ordered it and it returned.

Then I said, "O Prophet of Allah, I am the first to believe in you and to acknowledge that the tree did what it did just now with the command of Allah, the Sublime, in testimony to your Prophethood and to exalt your word. Upon this all the people shouted, "Rather a sorcerer, a liar; it is wonderful sorcery, he is very adept in it. Only a man like this (pointing to me) can stand testimony to you in your affairs."[1]

That is why the story of the moving of the tree at the command of the Holy Prophet (s) which is narrated by Imam Ali (a) as well as Waraqa ibn Naufal does not happen to be more than a miracle.

In books of traditions and history etc, hundreds of miracle of the Prophet of Islam (s) are recorded, which are sufficient to testify for him. Though we do not claim that all the miracles attributed to the Holy Prophet (s) are absolute and undoubted; they include some true miracles also which are sufficient to prove the original miracle. These miracles at least are not less than the miracles attributed to Musa and Isa (a) as they are considered as proofs to prove their ministry.

It can be concluded from the Holy Quran and books of history that Prophet Muhammad (s) was labeled as a magician and a madman because it is known that he performed extraordinary acts, which are usually accomplished through magic; but since we know that he was not a magician, it is understood that such acts were nothing but miracles.

At the end of this discussion, we feel it is necessary to say that miracles are extraordinary acts, which prophets employ in necessary circumstances to prove their prophethood. Therefore the prophet does not perform miracles at the

---

[1] *Nahjul Balagha*, Sermon 192

desire of those who look for excuses. The prophet is not a juggler or a show man that he should perform amazing acts to entertain the audience; on the contrary, he is the messenger of God sent to convey the life-giving message to the people and to guide them to salvation.

More than anything else, people should pay attention to his rightfulness, trustworthiness and his detailed program although he is also having miracle, but he uses them only to exhaust the proof and to prove his prophethood. But after that it is not necessary for him to repeat his miracles in every instance that excuse seekers demand.

More important is the fact that the Holy Quran is itself introduced to be an everlasting miracle and which is at the disposal of all. In spite of this, some people due to malice and excuse seekers refused to accept Islam and made allegations that the Prophet of Islam (s) was a sorcerer and a madman. Such people asked Prophet Muhammad (s) in selfishness: In case we accept your call, would you perform such and such extraordinary act? In such instances it is not necessary to display miracle as the Quran has also mentioned the demand of the polytheists from the Holy Prophet (s) and said:

قُل لَّئِنِ ٱجْتَمَعَتِ ٱلْإِنسُ وَٱلْجِنُّ عَلَىٰٓ أَن يَأْتُوا۟ بِمِثْلِ هَٰذَا ٱلْقُرْءَانِ لَا يَأْتُونَ بِمِثْلِهِۦ وَلَوْ كَانَ بَعْضُهُمْ لِبَعْضٍ ظَهِيرًا ۝ وَلَقَدْ صَرَّفْنَا لِلنَّاسِ فِى هَٰذَا ٱلْقُرْءَانِ مِن كُلِّ مَثَلٍ فَأَبَىٰٓ أَكْثَرُ ٱلنَّاسِ إِلَّا كُفُورًا ۝ وَقَالُوا۟ لَن نُّؤْمِنَ لَكَ حَتَّىٰ تَفْجُرَ لَنَا مِنَ ٱلْأَرْضِ يَنۢبُوعًا ۝ أَوْ تَكُونَ لَكَ جَنَّةٌ مِّن نَّخِيلٍ وَعِنَبٍ فَتُفَجِّرَ ٱلْأَنْهَٰرَ خِلَٰلَهَا تَفْجِيرًا ۝ أَوْ تُسْقِطَ ٱلسَّمَآءَ كَمَا زَعَمْتَ عَلَيْنَا كِسَفًا أَوْ تَأْتِىَ بِٱللَّهِ وَٱلْمَلَٰٓئِكَةِ قَبِيلًا ۝ أَوْ يَكُونَ لَكَ بَيْتٌ مِّن زُخْرُفٍ أَوْ تَرْقَىٰ فِى ٱلسَّمَآءِ وَلَن نُّؤْمِنَ لِرُقِيِّكَ حَتَّىٰ تُنَزِّلَ عَلَيْنَا كِتَٰبًا

نَّقْرَؤُهُۥ ۚ قُلْ سُبْحَانَ رَبِّى هَلْ كُنتُ إِلَّا بَشَرًا رَّسُولًا ۞

"Say: If men and jinn should combine together to bring the like of this Quran, they could not bring the like of it, though some of them were aiders of others. And certainly We have explained for men in this Quran every kind of similitude, but most men do not consent to aught but denying. And they say: We will by no means believe in you until you cause a fountain to gush forth from the earth for us. Or you should have a garden of palms and grapes in the midst of which you should cause rivers to flow forth, gushing out. Or you should cause the heaven to come down upon us in pieces as you think, or bring Allah and the angels face to face (with us). Or you should have a house of gold, or you should ascend into heaven, and we will not believe in your ascending until you bring down to us a book which we may read. Say: Glory be to my Lord; am I aught but a mortal apostle?" (17:88-93)

In the above mentioned verse, in the beginning the Quran is introduced as an everlasting miracle, which men and jinn cannot bring. After that it announces the demands of the opponents. Since the enemies, in spite of the fact that they themselves could not perform such acts, they belittled those miraculous acts and demanded other things as conditions for acceptance of faith; for example they said: We would accept your call if you can split the earth and bring out a spring of water from it, or that you bring for us orchards of fruits in which streams of water flow and things like that. They demanded such things from the Holy Prophet (s) who was told to reply to them as follow: Glorified is my Lord. I am a human being and nothing more. I have been sent from God to you in order to convey His commands.

QURAN – AN EVERLASTING MIRACLE

The Holy Quran is the most important miracle of the Prophet of Islam and the best proof of his prophethood. This great miracle is having superiority on all the other miracles from the following aspects:

1. It is permanent and everlasting and it has been given into the charge of man forever and they can witness the miracle of Quran throughout history. As opposed to other miracles, which endure only for a limited period of time.

2. It is also not limited from the aspect of space; it is under the control of one and all in every period of time, so that he may realize that it is a miracle, as opposed to other miracles that can be verified in a particular place and only some people are able to witness them.

3. The Quran, in addition to the fact that it is a proof of prophethood, is also a program of life and a guide to the right path, as opposed to other miracles, which do not have such an excellence.

The Holy Quran is the word of God and a miracle in such a way that others are incapable of presenting such a discourse. Quran introduces itself to be a miracle and by way of challenge says:

$$\text{قُل لَّئِنِ ٱجْتَمَعَتِ ٱلْإِنسُ وَٱلْجِنُّ عَلَىٰٓ أَن يَأْتُوا۟ بِمِثْلِ هَٰذَا ٱلْقُرْءَانِ لَا يَأْتُونَ بِمِثْلِهِۦ}$$

$$\text{وَلَوْ كَانَ بَعْضُهُمْ لِبَعْضٍ ظَهِيرًا ۝}$$

"Say: If men and jinn should combine together to bring the like of this Quran, they could not bring the like of it, though some of them were aiders of others." (17:88)

$$\text{أَمْ يَقُولُونَ ٱفْتَرَىٰهُ ۖ قُلْ فَأْتُوا۟ بِعَشْرِ سُوَرٍ مِّثْلِهِۦ مُفْتَرَيَٰتٍ وَٱدْعُوا۟ مَنِ ٱسْتَطَعْتُم}$$

$$\text{مِّن دُونِ ٱللَّهِ إِن كُنتُمْ صَٰدِقِينَ ۝ فَإِلَّمْ يَسْتَجِيبُوا۟ لَكُمْ فَٱعْلَمُوٓا۟ أَنَّمَآ أُنزِلَ بِعِلْمِ}$$

$$\text{ٱللَّهِ وَأَن لَّآ إِلَٰهَ إِلَّا هُوَ ۖ فَهَلْ أَنتُم مُّسْلِمُونَ ۝}$$

"Or, do they say: He has forged it. Say: Then bring ten forged chapters like it and call upon whom you can besides Allah, if you are truthful. But if they do not answer you, then know that it is revealed by Allah's knowledge and that there is no god but He; will you then submit?" (11:13-14)

$$\text{وَإِن كُنتُمْ فِى رَيْبٍ مِّمَّا نَزَّلْنَا عَلَىٰ عَبْدِنَا فَأْتُوا۟ بِسُورَةٍ مِّن مِّثْلِهِۦ وَٱدْعُوا۟}$$

$$\text{شُهَدَآءَكُم مِّن دُونِ ٱللَّهِ إِن كُنتُمْ صَٰدِقِينَ ۝ فَإِن لَّمْ تَفْعَلُوا۟ وَلَن تَفْعَلُوا۟ فَٱتَّقُوا۟}$$

$$\text{ٱلنَّارَ ٱلَّتِى وَقُودُهَا ٱلنَّاسُ وَٱلْحِجَارَةُ ۖ أُعِدَّتْ لِلْكَٰفِرِينَ ۝}$$

"And if you are in doubt as to that which We have revealed to Our servant, then produce a chapter like it and call on your witnesses besides Allah if you are truthful. But if you do (it) not and never shall you do (it), then be on your guard against the fire of which men and stones are the fuel; it is prepared for the unbelievers." (2:23-24)

In the above verses, Quran has been introduced as the miracle and proof of the veracity of the claim of Prophet

Muhammad (ṣ) and it has openly demanded from the people that if they have any doubt in the miracle of the Quran or the messengership of The Holy Prophet Muhammad (ṣ), they should bring a like of it or ten chapters or at least one chapter.

If those who are inimical to Islam had the capacity to perform this feat, they would have definitely taken up the challenge or at least brought one chapter like that of Quran and presented it to the Holy Prophet (ṣ) and Muslims in order to render the prophethood of His Eminence doubtful. This was the best method of confronting and defeating Islam. Therefore, if they had been able to perform this feat, they would have prevented the spread of the influence of Islam and succeeded in dispersing the new converts from the company of The Holy Prophet Muhammad (ṣ) and this also did not carry the bloodshed and difficulties of fighting battles.

But it is not mentioned anywhere in history that they took up this challenge of Quran and succeeded in it.

In any case, the challenge of the Quran is not restricted to the people contemporary to the period of the Messenger of Allah (ṣ), it is general and addressed to all the people of every age and place; it has asked all the intellectuals and litterateurs that if they have doubt in the messengership of The Holy Prophet Muhammad (ṣ) they should bring a like of this Quran or a chapter like it. But as the Quran predicted, they have till date not been able to perform this feat. Enemies of Islam have also written books in refutation of Quran and tried to insult it, but so far no one has succeeded in writing a book like it.

In the words of Almighty Allah, there is a beautiful fluency and attraction in it, which is not present in other books. It is from this aspect that it has severely influenced the pure and enlightened consciences. A large number of people in the early period of Islam were attracted by hearing the verses of Quran and they accepted Islam because of this. Numerous examples of such persons are mentioned in the history of Islam. Such was the extent of the attraction of Quran that it even confounded and attracted the enemies of Islam and even they had to confess that it is extraordinary. Below we present some instances of this:

Abul Fida writes: Walid Ibn Mughira came to the Messenger of Allah (ṣ) and the Prophet recited the Quran before him in such a way that he became inclined to Islam. This information reached Abu Jahl and he came to him and said: Uncle, your relatives intend to collect money for you. What for, he asked. He replied: So that they may hand it over to you, because you had gone to Muhammad to get something. Walid said: Quraish know that I am the richest of all of them. Abu Jahl said: So issue a statement that may reach your relatives and they may come to know that you are a denier of Muhammad. Walid said: What shall I say? By God, none of you is more learned than me about poetry and Arab human and Jinn literature. By God, the Quran of Muhammad does not resemble any of these. By God, the discourse of Muhammad has sweetness, beauty and attraction; branches of the discourse of Muhammad have fructified and his roots are being watered. His discourse is having precedence over other discourses and no discourse is superior to his.

Abu Jahl said to Walid: Your kin will not be pleased with you unless you make a statement with regard to this matter. He said: Give me sometime to consider it. After thinking about it for sometime, he said: The discourse of Muhammad is magical as it has the ability to bewitch others.[1]

Jabir Ibn Abdullah says: One day Quraish gathered and said: We should procure a man, who is most learned of all in magic, soothsaying and poetry and send to this man who has created dissension among us and who talks ill of our religion, so that he may speak to him. All said: We do not know of anyone better than Utbah Ibn Rabia. Therefore this assignment was given to Utbah.

Utbah came to the Messenger of Allah (ṣ) and asked: Who is better, you or your father? The Messenger of Allah (ṣ) did not give any reply. He asked again: Who is better, you or Abdul Muttalib? Again the Messenger of Allah (ṣ) did not accord any reply. Utbah said: If you think they were better than you, they worshipped the same idols that you talk ill of; and if you consider yourself to be better than them, say something that we might hear. By Allah, I have not seen any lamb more inauspicious than you, you have created disunity among us and criticized our religion and degraded us among the Arabs in such a way that they say: A magician has appeared among Quraish and we fear him that he would cause war among us and destroy all of us.

O man, if you want wealth, we can collect so much wealth for you that you would become the richest of Quraish and if you are need of a spouse, we can get you married to any lady you want.

---

[1] *Al-Bidaya wan Nihaya*, Vol. 3, Pg. 78

At this moment the Holy Prophet (s) asked Utbah: Have you said all you wanted to say? Yes. He said: Then listen:

$$\text{بِسْمِ اللّٰهِ الرَّحْمٰنِ الرَّحِيْمِ}$$

$$\text{تَنْزِيْلٌ مِنَ الرَّحْمٰنِ الرَّحِيْمِ ۞ كِتَابٌ فُصِّلَتْ آيَاتُهُ قُرْآنًا عَرَبِيًّا لِقَوْمٍ يَعْلَمُوْنَ ۞}$$

"In the name of Allah, the Beneficent, the Merciful. 41.1. Ha Mim! A revelation from the Beneficent, the Merciful God: A Book of which the verses are made plain, an Arabic Quran for a people who know." (41:1-3)

...till he came to the verse:

$$\text{فَإِنْ أَعْرَضُوْا فَقُلْ أَنْذَرْتُكُمْ صَاعِقَةً مِثْلَ صَاعِقَةِ عَادٍ وَثَمُوْدَ ۞}$$

"But if they turn aside, then say: I have warned you of a scourge like the scourge of Ad and Thamood." (41:13)

Utbah said: Enough, do you have anything else? No, he replied.

After this Utbah returned to Quraish and they asked him: What did you do? He replied: I spoke to Muhammad. They asked: What did he say in reply? Utbah said: By the one who established the Kaaba, I did not understand anything from the discourse of Muhammad, except that he threatened you with lightning as in the case of Aad and Thamud. They asked: An Arab spoke to you and you did not understand him? He replied: Yes, I did not understand anything, except the mention of lightning.[1]

---

[1] *Al-Bidaya wan Nihaya*, Vol. 3, Pg. 80

According to another narration, Utbah said: I have heard such a discourse from this man that I have not heard anything like it from anyone else.[1]

According to yet another version, Utbah said: By Allah, I have not heard such a discourse from anyone else so far, neither in poetry nor soothsaying; O people of Quraish, leave this man to his own devices, his discourse is having a great future. If Arabs accept it, it will be sufficient for you and if he is able to conquer the Arabs, his kingdom and honor would be your kingdom and honor and you would benefit from him most of all. Quraish said in reply: Muhammad has bewitched you through his tongue.[2]

Aspects of the miracle of Quran

Previously it was mentioned that Quran is a miracle and it is different from human discourse. Friends and enemies have also confessed to this. At this point, it is necessary to explain the causes of its miraculousness. Scholar, theologians, litterateurs and commentators of Quran have mentioned some aspects in this regard and we shall mention some of them here:

A New Style

It is learnt from a close study of Quran that this great book is having a fresh lightness and it is completely different from the style and diction of other writings. Verses of Quran are not poetic couplets, because it is not composed on poetic meters and also does not have rhymes. Moreover, poetry is mostly imaginative and based on hyperbole, whereas the verses of Quran are not so.

---

[1] *Al-Bidaya wan Nihaya*, Vol. 3, Pg. 82
[2] *Al-Bidaya wan Nihaya*, Vol. 3, Pg. 82

Although Quran is not a book of poetry, each of its verses are like coherent couplets along with a special flow and style arranged in a systematic way and between the end of every chapter there is a particular symmetry and similarity which imparts appeal and beauty to it. The verses do not have the meter of couplets, but they have remarkable compatibility and appeal.

Quran is arranged as a soft prose, but it is different from other prose in two ways:

A. It is at an elevated level from the aspect of eloquence and clarity, selection of words and sentences. It has mentioned the most complex points in an extremely easy and suitable words, which though simple and sweet are also meaningful, whereas such a thing is not found in other discourses. So much so that even the sermons, traditions and supplications of the Holy Prophet (s) do not have such appeal. Although Amirul Momineen (a), was considered to be the most eloquent of the Arabs and he became familiar with Quran during his childhood; he knew it by heart and had written it with his hands, and his *Nahjul Balagha* is considered as the most eloquent of the books; in spite of that it does not have the same appeal and beauty of the Holy Quran. Verses of Quran that occasionally appear within the sermons of *Nahjul Balagha* or traditions shine like stars in the sky.

B. Matters of the Holy Quran have a special style and arrangement, which is a remarkable difference with other books. In this heavenly book, there are different subjects like knowing God, resurrection, Judgment Day, accounting, Paradise and Hell, prophethood and stories, effects of good and bad character, creation of the earth, sky, man, animals, vegetation, sea, cloud, winds, rain and rules and regulations, lawful and unlawful actions, worship acts, transactions, marriage and divorce, penalties, retaliations and blood monies, advices and moral lessons and many such topics.

Such topics and their like are spread throughout the Quran under various topics. But it is not thus in other books, since every book deals only with one particular topic and different topics related to the main subject are discussed. Sometimes, some other topics are also discussed, but some topics are also discussed separately. Such a book is in fact a number of books each of which follows a single aim.

But Quran has not discussed only one subject; on the contrary, it has not even discussed all the problems related to a number of different subjects at one and the same place together. It has mentioned different aspects in a scattered way; they are placed besides each other, but they are not incoherent and asymmetrical; on the contrary they have a special symmetry that keeps them connected to each other and which shapes the verses and chapters. Different subjects of Quran are like different priceless gems arranged in a special manner.

That is why the Holy Quran in the arrangement of its subject matter does not resemble any of the books of morals, legal, anecdotal, scientific knowledge, humanities, literature and history; but each of them is connected to others and they are all harmonious. The aim of Quran includes: The cognition of man, world, Almighty Allah, resurrection and life after death and also calling man to worship the one God and inviting him to fulfill the social and individual duties and purification and training of the self from bad manners and morals, development of the self by perfection of morals and finally, proximity to God and wayfaring on the path of God.

Decisiveness in discourse

Subject matter of the Quran is mentioned with clarity and decisiveness in such a way that it has permeated into the depths of the soul of man and the hearer feels that the speaker is witnessing reality and is giving information from the unseen. It is from this aspect that the prophecies of the Quran inspire hope and its threats are severely pounding.

Contemplation on the verses of Quran polishes the soul of man and raises him above the world of matter and makes him familiar with the unseen world. Therefore, it is possible for the soul of man to witness realities in these emotions, which their eyes cannot see. Appeal of the verses of Quran is to such an extent that opponents of Islam labeled them as magic. Sometimes, by hearing them, they were so bewildered that automatically they did not understand how to justify them. It was mentioned before also that Utbah was so bewildered on hearing the verses of Surah Fussilat that he expressed helplessness in justifying and explaining the verses and in reply to Quraish said: "I did not understand anything, except that he threatened with a lightning like the lightning of Aad and Thamud."

Fearing this same ideal appeal, the leaders of polytheism said to people: Do not give ear to the words of Muhammad, because it is possible that you would be deceived.

Ibn Athir writes: Tufayl Ibn Amr Doosi, who was a man from a noble family and also an accomplished poet, says: I traveled to Mecca during the period the Messenger of Allah (ṣ) and stayed there for sometime. Some Quraish elders approached me and said: O Tufayl, you have come to our city at a time when this man (The Holy Prophet Muhammad) is living here. He has cast us into hardships and has created discord among us. His discourse, like magic and sorcery, causes separation between father and son, wife and husband and brothers. Therefore, we fear that you might also be deceived. So do not speak a word to Muhammad and do not give ear to his talks.

Tufayl says: So much they emphasized this point that I became determined that I would not hear the words of Muhammad or speak to him, and I also stuffed cotton wool into my ears.

In the morning I went to the Holy Mosque and saw the Messenger of Allah (ṣ) reciting prayers near the Kaaba. I went nearer; Allah had intended that his discourse would reach my ears. A beautiful discourse reached my ears. I said to myself: May your mother mourn for you, you are a poet and an intellectual and know well how to discriminate between good and bad. Thus what restrains you from hearing the statements of this man? If it is good and proper you should accept it and if it is evil and invalid, you can leave it.

Tufayl says: I waited a little while till Muhammad departed to his house, and then I followed him, when he entered the house, I also entered. At that moment I said: O Muhammad, leaders of Quraish told me this and that, but Allah intended that your discourse should reach my ears. I heard your beautiful discourse, tell me what is your aim and objective? So Muhammad presented Islam to me and recited the Quran. By Allah, I had not heard any discourse more beautiful and a matter more definite.[1]

Therefore, if you also had been conversant with Arab literature and interpretation of Quran, contemplated on the fresh style of its arrangement of verses and selection of words and the lofty subjects that Quran has chosen to express in those words and the construction of sentences, you will also discover some amazing aspects of the elegance of this heavenly book.

No contradiction between the verses

Another sign of the miraculousness of Quran is that there is no contradiction between its verses. Quran itself has highlighted this point and said:

$$\text{أَفَلَا يَتَدَبَّرُونَ ٱلْقُرْءَانَ وَلَوْ كَانَ مِنْ عِنْدِ غَيْرِ ٱللَّهِ لَوَجَدُوا فِيهِ ٱخْتِلَٰفًا كَثِيرًا ﴿٨٢﴾}$$

"Do they not then meditate on the Quran? And if it were from any other than Allah, they would have found in it many a discrepancy." (4:82)

The above verse has reprimanded and said: Why do you not contemplate on the Quran so that you may understand that its verses have no contradiction and that they are revealed from Almighty Allah, because the discourse of man is not without contradiction.

Two kinds of contradictions are seen in books written by human beings and none of them is present in Quran.

---

[1] *Usud al-Ghaba,* Vol. 3, Pg. 54

First: Contradictions related to subtlety, choice of words, style and diction, observance of literary aspects, eloquence and clarity.

Since man is under constant change and perfection, as much as he writes and practices, as much expert he becomes and as much his writing improves and becomes more eloquent and beautiful. In the same way, different personal conditions, mood, different incidents and conditions of life, all of them affect the writing of a writer. Man in a condition of health or illness, joy or indisposition, happiness or sorrow, feeling of victory or defeat, exaltation or feeling of humiliation, cannot write in the same way and each of them affect his writing and beauty of discourse.

That is why if you study a book with attention you would realize that its different sections are not same from the aspect of beauty and elegance and the only book, which does not have such differences is the Holy Quran; neither the chapters revealed first have any difference with the last chapters nor the middle chapters and its verses.

The Holy Quran was revealed on the Prophet of Islam throughout a period of twenty-three years, gradually in different space and time and in different conditions, but in spite of this, no difference is seen in its different sections from the aspect of eloquence and clarity or elegance of discourse; this proves that Quran is the discourse of God, which is not susceptible to change and development in His being or actions.

Second: Existence of incongruous and contradictory matter is certain in the writing of human beings. If an unlettered author dictates for 23 years matter on various subjects and different topics, such a book would without any doubt not be free of contractions.

It is possible for a writer to write something at one time and later as a result of having changed his opinion about something may write to the contrary; or it is possible that he might do this because of forgetfulness or carelessness. Moreover it is possible that another writer coming after him may refute his arguments and through innovative arguments criticize him. In many instances it is seen that preceding writers have written on different subjects using their evidences and argumentations, but after a passage of time other writers have refuted those theories through new methods.

History testifies that The Holy Prophet Muhammad (ṣ) did not attend any school.[1] In the Holy Quran also he is mentioned as the unlettered prophet.[2] All the verses and chapters of Quran were revealed to His Eminence (ṣ) in twenty-three years in various instances and in fragments.

His Eminence did not write down the verses of Quran himself, on the contrary he dictated them to others. He did not revise any of his previous statements in any way.

---

[1] *"And you did not recite before it any book, nor did you transcribe one with your right hand, for then could those who say untrue things have doubted." (29:48)*

[2] *"Those who follow the Apostle-Prophet, the unlettered, whom they find written down with them in the Taurat and the Injeel (who) enjoins them good and forbids them evil, and makes lawful to them the good things and makes unlawful to them impure things, and removes from them their burden and the shackles which were upon them; so (as for) those who believe in him and honor him and help him, and follow the light which has been sent down with him, these it is that are the successful." (7:157)*

In spite of this, not the slightest contradiction or incompatibility is seen in the verses of Quran.

Instances cannot arise in rules and regulations related to society, rights and worship acts of Quran, which are not compatible to the religious and moral basis of that heavenly book. Nothing appears in problems related to morals, which is contradictory to the religious basis. In the stories of Quran and the biographies of the prophets and the past nations nothing is seen that is opposed to the fundamentals of belief or morals. As regards problems connected to nature, nothing is seen which is opposed to the basics of thoughts. In points related to resurrection and rewards and punishment of the hereafter there is nothing incompatible to justice and perfection of Almighty Allah. With regard to points about general and special prophethood nothing is mentioned which is opposed to the principles of divine cognition.

Hence, although Quran has spoken about a number of different subjects, all of them are organized and compatible and do not have the smallest incompatibility between themselves. Therefore they cannot be a product of human beings. On the contrary, it is the discourse of God revealed on the heart of the Prophet of Islam and no one else can bring such a piece of writing.

Information of the Unseen

The Holy Quran has informed about some events that were to occur in the future and this itself is considered to be a miraculous aspect, because it is not possible for ordinary human beings to get this knowledge. Below we shall mention some predictions issued by the Holy Quran:

The Holy Quran says:

الٓمٓ ۝ غُلِبَتِ ٱلرُّومُ ۝ فِىٓ أَدْنَى ٱلْأَرْضِ وَهُم مِّنۢ بَعْدِ غَلَبِهِمْ سَيَغْلِبُونَ ۝ فِى بِضْعِ سِنِينَ ۗ لِلَّهِ ٱلْأَمْرُ مِن قَبْلُ وَمِنۢ بَعْدُ ۚ وَيَوْمَئِذٍ يَفْرَحُ ٱلْمُؤْمِنُونَ ۝ بِنَصْرِ ٱللَّهِ ۚ يَنصُرُ مَن يَشَآءُ ۖ وَهُوَ ٱلْعَزِيزُ ٱلرَّحِيمُ ۝ وَعْدَ ٱللَّهِ ۖ لَا يُخْلِفُ ٱللَّهُ وَعْدَهُۥ وَلَٰكِنَّ أَكْثَرَ ٱلنَّاسِ لَا يَعْلَمُونَ ۝

"Alif Lam Mim. The Romans are vanquished, in a near land, and they, after being vanquished, shall overcome, within a few years. Allah's is the command before and after; and on that day the believers shall rejoice, with the help of Allah; He helps whom He pleases; and He is the Mighty, the Merciful; (This is) Allah's promise! Allah will not fail His promise, but most people do not know. (30:1-6)

From this verse, it can be concluded that in the early period of Islam, defeat and hardships would befall the soldiers of Rome. This event occurred near the land of Hijaz and the Arabs of the Arabian Peninsula, especially the new converts to Islam, became very much disconcerted at the defeat of the Romans. The above verse was revealed at that time informing the Muslims that after this defeat, in a short period of less than ten years, the Romans would overcome their enemies and believers would become pleased with the help of God.

The prediction of Quran proved true and within that stipulated time the Romans, who were the People of Book conquered Persia; believers were also pleased by this victory.

It is necessary to mention about the political and administrative conditions of the two great powers of that time (Rome and Iran) and the clashes that they had with each other in order to fully understand this important event of history:

Before the advent of Islam, two great imperial powers ruled in Asia and the neighborhood of Arabian lands: One was Iran, which had a huge land mass under its control, which was much larger than present Iran. Another power was that of the Romans, whose kingdom stretched up to Egypt and Syria.

These two powers were always engaged in a struggle of expansion of their boundaries and power and were all the time in confrontation with each other. Sometimes one of them considered his opponent as weak and attacked him and seized some of his territory and wealth and plundered those places. After some time the defeated party would regain its power and then take up arms against the other and re-conquer the areas that had been seized from it before. This conflict continued forever between these two opponents.

Arabs of the surrounding areas were also not safe as a result of the confrontation of the two adversaries. The capital of the rulers from the family of Lakham in the city of Hira (near Kufa) who were under overlordship of the Sasanid rulers, who had ruled for many years. Their reign continued till around 602 A.D. At that time Khosrow Parvez decided to annex their kingdom and join it to his dominion.[1] When a Sasanid king became aware that the Himyar king intends to secede from the Sasanid domination, he sent a huge army in 598 A.D. to southern

---

[1] *Tarikh Iran Az Salukian taa Furupashi daulat Sasani*, Vol. 3, Pg. 263

Arabia, which was able to vanquish them after a severe fight and south Arabia became a province of the Sasanid kingdom.[1] On the other hand, the Roman kingdoms also gave business to south Arabia and helped that country in opposing their adversaries, because many Christians had settled down in those territories.

That is why the people of the Arabian Peninsula were affected by the victory or defeat of each of these two opponents. When the Sasanids gained victory, the Christians of Arabia became despondent and the polytheists were elated, since they considered the Iranians to be their co-religionists as both of them were fire worshippers, so they considered their victory as their own victory.

On the other hand, when the Romans were victorious, the Christians of Arabia became elated, but the polytheists were aggrieved as they sensed danger. Now we shall explain the main points:

The Prophet of Islam (ṣ) was vested with the office of prophethood in 610 A.D. in Mecca. From 602 to 610 A.D. it was a very bad period for the Roman power, because as result of civil disturbance and internal strife, it had become absolutely weak. During this time Khosrow Parvez, the Sasanid king discovered the weakness of the Roman Empire; so he took advantage of the circumstances and launched fierce attack on his opponent. These attacks began from 610 and continued till 619 A.D. The strong Sasanid fighters gained remarkable victories one after another.

---

[1] *Tarikh Iran Az Salukian taa Furupashi daulat Sasani*, Vol. 3, Pg. 256

From 605 to 613 A.D. cities like: Dara, Aaamad, Adsaa, Nasirapolis, Aleppo, Apaya and Damascus fell under the domination of the Sasanids.

Khosrow Parvez became arrogant as a result of his remarkable victories and he declared a holy war against the Christians. Some Jew groups also joined ranks with him. In the year 614 he attacked Jerusalem and killed around 90000 Christians and plundered the city. He razed and burnt down a number of churches. During these attacks they seized and brought to Iran the crucifix that was considered by the Christians to be the original and was the most venerated emblem of their faith. Parvez wrote to Hercules the Roman Emperor:

From Khosrow Parvez, the greatest Lord and master of the rulers of the earth to Hercules, a worthless servant who is ignorant of himself, you say that you trust in God, but why did He did not save Jerusalem from my hands?

In the year 616, Khosrow sent a huge army to Alexandria and in 619 he conquered Egypt. His sent another army to Asia Minor and occupied Chaldea in 617.[1]

Rapid and wide ranging Sasanid victories were really remarkable from different aspects. Some information of these victories reached the people of Arabia who lived in the surrounding lands. The reaction of Arabs to these reports used to be of two kinds: Polytheists used to be elated at them, because they considered their victory as victory against forces of monotheism. But Christians were aggrieved and they feared their safety and peace.

---

[1] Will Durant, *History of Civilization*, Part I, Vol. 4, Pg. 181; *Tarikh Iran Az Salukian taa Furupashi daulat Sasani*, Vol. 3, Pg. 264-265

Muslims of the early period of Islam who were very few in numbers, and were usually persecuted and oppressed by polytheists, used to be extremely wary of the rapid and remarkable victories of the Sasanids. Moreover, they also feared that Arabia would also come under their subjugation. Because the enemy has reached up to 'Azrat' which is mentioned in Quran as 'Adnal arz' and they were extremely fearful of the oncoming danger.

The above verse was revealed with regard to these circumstances and it gave glad tidings to Muslims that in a period of less than ten years, the soldiers of Rome would vanquish the Persians and the believers would become elated at the divine help.

Ibn Athir writes: 'Adnal Arz' implies the land of Azrat since it is an Arab land closest to Byzantine territories and the Romans in some battles had retreated to this area. The Prophet of Islam and Muslims were aggrieved at the victory of Persians over the Romans, since the Romans were People of the Book and the infidels were pleased at these victories and considered the Majus like their own selves. When this verse was revealed, Abu Bakr laid a bet for a hundred camels with Ubayy ibn Khalaf, although at that time betting was not unlawful.[1]

Muslims became hopeful of the divine promise and began to count the days for its realization. At last the promise of God was fulfilled and the Romans gained victory over the Persians.

It is mentioned in history that the Roman Emperor, Hercules I was extremely aggrieved at the defeat at the

---

[1] *Al-Kamil fit Tarikh*, Vol. 1, Pg. 479

hands of Persians and decided to strengthen his weak points and take serious steps to regain the territories lost to their opponents. With this aim, he took reformative steps and corrections and prepared his men to launch a severe and widespread attack. In 622 A.D. he sent a powerful naval force through the Black Sea in Armenis to attack the Persians from the rear. The next year he attacked Azerbaijan and plundered the birth place of Zoroaster and extinguished their holy fire, which had been burning since ages. They recovered the holy crucifix from the Persians and returned it to Jerusalem.[1]

Although Romans were defeated at Azraat (Adnal Arz) in 613 A.D., they continued repeated and formidable attacks on Persians till year 622 A.D. when they were finally victorious. That is they gained victory in nine years after their defeat as mentioned in the Holy Quran as "Within a few years". That is why the prediction of Quran when it said: second victory of Romans would occur in a period of less than ten years after their defeat, proved true. At that time, Christians and Muslims were elated at the new victory of Romans over the Persians.

Realization of this divine promise is an evidence of the miraculous aspect of Quran.[2]

---

[1] *Tarikh Iran Az Salukian taa Furupashi daulat Sasani*, Vol. 3, Pg. 266; Will Durant, *History of Civilization*, Part I, Vol. 4, Pg. 182

[2] Historians of Islam like Tabari, Ibne Athir, Abul Fida and others, and in the same way commentators of Quran are having unanimity that the promise of the Holy Quran was finally fulfilled and the Romans after their defeat were able to overpower the Persians and the gap between this defeat and victory was less than ten years, but regretfully the accurate time of defeat and victory is not recorded in history. In Islamic sources, it is mentioned that the victory of

Romans occurred during the time of the Battle of Badr (2 A.H.) or at the time of Battle of Hudaibiyah (6 A.H.), but both these times do not tally with the prophecy of Quran because their defeat in 613 A.D. corresponds to the third year of Hijra which is 13 and 16 years respectively from Battle of Badr and Battle of Hudaibiyah. While the prophecy of Quran is that the victory of the Romans would be in less than ten years. Hence, none of these two dates tally with the prophecy of Quran, but what is mentioned in the books of the history of Iran is absolutely accurate. And hence we should accept that the victory of Romans occurred around the year 13 A.H.

MUHAMMAD, THE LAST PROPHET

The Holy Prophet Muhammad (ṣ) is the last of the divine prophets. After His Eminence, no other prophet is going to be sent by God. The Prophet of Islam, from the beginning of his mission, introduced himself as the seal of the prophets and was accepted by the Muslims as such. The subject of finality of prophethood in the Islamic milieu is considered to be an important matter and it is not in need of evidence.

Finality is mentioned in the Holy Quran as well as books of traditions. It is mentioned in Quran that:

مَّا كَانَ مُحَمَّدٌ أَبَآ أَحَدٍ مِّن رِّجَالِكُمْ وَلَـٰكِن رَّسُولَ ٱللَّهِ وَخَاتَمَ ٱلنَّبِيِّـۧنَ ۗ وَكَانَ ٱللَّهُ بِكُلِّ شَىْءٍ عَلِيمًا ۝

"Muhammad is not the father of any of your men, but he is the Apostle of Allah and the Last of the prophets; and Allah is cognizant of all things." (33:40)

If the Arabic word of KH-T-M is recited with vowel 'I' on 'T', as some reciters have done this, it would imply one who ends something; thus it clearly shows that The Holy Prophet Muhammad (ṣ) is the last of the prophets. But if it is recited with the vowel 'A' on 'T' it denotes a thing with which something ends. Ring and seal are also called as such, because they are placed at the end of a letter and indicate the end of it. According to the second possibility also, it is concluded from the verse that the Holy Prophet (ṣ) is the last prophet, because he is introduced as a seal, which has come at the end of the letter of prophethood.

Therefore, no other prophet is to appear after him. Thus the finality of the Prophet of Islam is nicely concluded from the above verse as the Muslims of the early period of Islam also understood it in this meaning and did not have any doubt in the finality of the prophethood of His Eminence.

Other verses also exist in this regard, but there is no need to mention them here.

A large number of traditions also exist with regard to finality of prophethood and some of them are mentioned below:

Saad Ibn Abi Waqqas has narrated from his father that the Messenger of Allah (ṣ) said to Imam Ali (a):

You are to me as Harun was to Musa (a), except that there is no prophet after me.[1]

The above tradition is known as "the tradition of position" (*Hadith Manzila*) and is recorded in Shia and Sunni books through various channels and it proves that no other prophet is to come after the Prophet of Islam.

It is narrated from Abu Huraira that he said:

The Messenger of Allah (ṣ) said: I have been sent for all the people of the world and prophethood has ended with me.[2] Abu Amama has narrated from the Holy Prophet (ṣ) that he said:

---

[1] *Sahih Muslim*, Vol. 4, Pg. 1870
[2] *At-Tabaqatul Kubra*, Vol. 1, Pg. 192

> *O people, no prophet is to come after me and there is no nation (Ummah) after you. So worship Allah, perform the five daily ritual prayers, observe the fasts of the month of Ramadan, perform the Hajj of Kaaba and pay the Zakat of your wealth, so that your selves are purified. Also obey the ones who are vested with authority among you so that you may enter Paradise.*[1]

Amirul Momineen (a) said:

> *Almighty Allah sent the Holy Prophet (ṣ) at a time when no prophet existed on the earth and there was a time gap between them and discord had developed among the people. Thus by sending him, He ended prophethood and revelation came to an end.*[2]

It is concluded from his tradition and others like it that The Holy Prophet Muhammad (ṣ) is the seal of prophets and that after him no other prophet came and nor any prophet is going to come. It was also stated previously that the Prophet of Islam, at the beginning of his mission, introduced himself as the seal of prophets and all those who accepted his prophethood they also accepted the finality of his prophethood. Therefore no separate evidence is required to prove the finality of the Prophet of Islam.

Question: What is the reason of the finality of prophethood? If people are in need of a prophet and heavenly commands, this need existed at all times and still exists. And if after the advent of Prophet of Islam this need does not exist anymore, with regard to the past

---

[1] *Wasailush Shia*, Vol. 1, Pg. 23

[2] *Nahjul Balagha*, Sermon 129

prophets also the same possibility was there. Why one of them were not considered as the seal of the prophets?

Reply: Some points are mentioned below:

1. Religion is a reality and a way and all heavenly religions are same in that regard. Principles of religion are explained in brief as follows:

First: Faith in God and His recognition. Second: Faith in resurrection and life after death and the rewards and punishments of the hereafter. Third: Faith in prophets. Fourth: Moral, worship and social duties and responsibilities of human beings.

All the prophets and all heavenly religions are similar in this regard and they called their followers to the same principles.

2. Although heavenly religions are similar in principles and generalities, they are not same on an equal level; on the contrary from the aspect of depth of religious cognition and intellectual matters, in social rules and regulations, in the condition and kind of worship rituals etc. they are very much different from each other. Religions have gradually developed and spread through the ages. The mentioned differences are effects of intellectual maturity and the level of knowledge of the people and the changes and transformations that occurred in the life of human beings.

Learning and intellectual capacity of the ancient people was definitely not at the level of the present man. And from the aspect of individual and social life also, the ancient man was in no way like the man of today. Religious knowledge, laws of faith and other matters were also sent by Almighty God to man through the channel of prophets in accordance to the capability of man and they spoke to people according their intellectual level. Therefore the Prophet of Islam (ṣ) said:

> *We prophets have been commanded to speak to people in accordance with their intellectual level.[1]*

Prophets through the ages, like loving parents held the hands of the people with determination and took them through development step by step till they reached the present level. Therefore as much man gained intellectual maturity as much advanced religious concepts were presented to him. And in the same way, if they were in need of more advanced rules and regulations they were given as much advanced rules and regulations.

Such advancement continued through the ages under the supervision and efforts of prophets till the time that the intellect and capacity of man reached to a level that he could understand the most complex religious concepts and knowledge; with this aim the Prophet of Islam was sent, so that he may remove this need of man.

The Holy Quran through the Prophet of Islam was revealed for the people so that it may convey to them the loftiest religious cognitions and realities and not only for the people of that time; on the contrary, the intellectuals of every age could benefit from it and they would never become old.

The Holy Quran and the life history of the Prophet of Islam are two religious and scientific heritages that are handed over to Muslims.

---

[1] *Tohufful Uqul*, Pg. 36

3. The Holy Prophet (ṣ) also made another arrangement to protect the knowledge of prophethood, laws of Islam and their application and that was through the appointment of Imam. The Prophet of Islam, by the order of Almighty Allah introduced the infallible Imams as reliable points of reference in intellectual and religious matters and Quranic sciences and considered their statements and manners as the final proof.

Therefore in this way also he entrusted the Muslims with numerous traditions to guarantee the fulfillment of their needs.

4. Permission to deduce laws of Shariah from the Holy Quran, traditions and life history of Infallibles (a) as well as the application of reason. Intellectuals and Islamic scholars in addition to the Holy Quran have at their disposal another great treasure, which are traditions through whom they can solve all the religious problems of man. In the same way is deductions based on the valuable sources of Islam and fulfillment of different needs of man throughout the changing times.

5. People of the time of the Prophet of Islam from the aspect of intellect had reached such a level that they were eligible to have been given the sciences of prophethood fully and that they can make efforts to protect and propagate them.

Muslims of the early period of Islam possessed this capability that they can protect their heavenly scripture and guard its writing from interpolation and forgery and preserve it for the future generations. In the same way, they had such intellectual maturity and possibilities that they acquired hundreds of thousands of traditions regarding various topics from the Holy Prophet (ṣ) and the Infallible Imams (a) and guarded them in all circumstances.

Therefore it was at such a special time having so many possibilities, that the Prophet of Islam was appointed as a prophet. He brought the Quran and he conveyed to the people the most advanced religious concepts and laws. He perfected the religion through Imamate and introduced the infallible Imams as guardians of faith and those who were to continue his path. With this program, the Islamic Ummah became self sufficient and it never became needful of a new prophet.

This is the philosophy of the finality of prophethood, but such possibilities were not available for the past prophets and nations.

Permanence of the laws of Islam and the changing life of man

Previously it was proved that the Prophet of Islam was the seal of the prophets and after him no other prophet is to come. At this point, it is possible that someone may pose frivolous objection and say: You consider laws of Islam as solution of all problems at all times, whereas the fact is that circumstances of man are always changing and new occurrences appear requiring new laws of religion. On other words, how can you justify the permanence of the laws of religion when the needs of life continue to change all the time?

How can the laws and rules of Islam, which were revealed 1420 years ago and were suitable for the life of the people of Arabian Peninsula, suit the developed life of the man of today? Therefore the complex and difficult life of today needs more advanced laws and rules. If man is in need of heavenly laws, it would have been better if there had been a new prophet in every age, so that he may bring a more perfect law as per the new needs.

In reply to this objection, it can be said that the needs of the life of man, which were the aim behind devising of laws and rules have two aspects: Permanence and change: The permanent aspect is from the creation and human nature and which originates from his natural instincts and talents and all men at all times and places are similar in this matter. For example, all human beings require nourishment, water, clothes and a shelter. In fact these natural needs are applicable to all human beings even though there might be great difference between them. As a result of this need man requires different types of exchanges like: buying and selling, rentals, liens and other transactions. Since human beings live in a society, they are needful of the help and cooperation of each other and even the civilized society is needful of right and perfect laws so that their application may guarantee the rights of all and that it may prevent oppression and excess.

Laws related to laborers and employers, ownership and its limits, sale and purchase, rent, pledges, justice and testimony, penalties, blood monies and retaliation etc. are shaped from these same natural needs.

Expression of sexual instincts also is a natural need and all human beings are needful of it. It is the same natural need, which has brought marriage and divorce into existence and which is the cause of legislation of laws related to matrimony and mutual rights between spouses, and between parents and children.

That is why the laws, which have come in the religious law of Islam, and which follow the natural instincts and needs of man, are all permanent and perpetual and they cannot have any problem with the finality of prophethood of the Holy Prophet (s).

With regard to the changing needs of man it can be said that with attention to the changing conditions of the world and ever-increasing scientific and technological development, inventions of various tools and gadgets of daily use, there will be suitable solutions and fresh laws as religion is answerable for them and the holy religious law of Islam saw two ways to solve this problem:

First method: Jurisprudence (*Ijtihad*): It was stated previously that Islam is a valuable heritage of knowledge, religious cognition and laws based on Quran and traditions that is left for Muslims. If the Islamic jurisprudents with attention to the demands of every age contemplate and research the sources of Islam, they can derive the appropriate solutions of the new problems and convey them to the people and may take the Islamic society on the path of progress along with different advanced societies of the world.

The Islamic scholar should be aware of present conditions and place and well versed with modern needs of the great human society; he should also be having a wide view of the world and must be broad minded; he should be able to find out the solution of new difficult problems from self sufficient religious sources of Islam and convey them to Muslims. And in this way he proves to the world that laws of Islam can be implemented in every time and place and they can guarantee the success of the world and the hereafter of its followers.

Second method – discretions of the jurist: It is automatically proved that governance is only according to rules and regulations of Islam. A large part of rules and regulations of Shariah are related to administration of society and political and social matters and their enforcement, without the existence of a religious, committed and expert ruler is not possible.

Muslim leaders have the responsibility to administer the Islamic government under the limits of the laws of Shariah and by complete application of the laws of Islam they can take it ahead of injustice and moral and social corruption and maintain Islamic justice. For governance of Islamic jurist it is a duty that he should make these arrangements in all conditions and times.

Although some Islamic laws are devised with this same aim and by applying them perfectly this aim can be achieved, but the jurist ruler sometimes has to face extraordinary and difficult circumstances in administering the territories of Islam as their solution requires authorities and special qualities and such discretions have been devised with foresight for Muslim rulers.

The Muslim ruler has permission to protect the principles and general sources of Islam and in observing the exigencies of Islamic nation, to frame rules and regulations and to use them in administration of the country. Such rules and regulations are called as the rules of governance.

The Holy Prophet (s) was having this power and he used them. After him the same powers are given to the Infallible Imams (a). Especially it is the same law that

Muslims are obliged to follow as per the orders of the Prophet and the Holy Imams (a) who are mentioned as "those vested with authority" (*Ulil Amr*).

The Holy Quran says:

يَٰٓأَيُّهَا ٱلَّذِينَ ءَامَنُوٓا۟ أَطِيعُوا۟ ٱللَّهَ وَأَطِيعُوا۟ ٱلرَّسُولَ وَأُو۟لِى ٱلۡأَمۡرِ مِنكُمۡ

"O you who believe! Obey Allah and obey the Apostle and those in authority from among you..." (4:59)

According to a large number of traditions narrated in our sources, the responsibility of governance during the period of the occultation of the Infallible Imam is given to the just religious scholar who has determination and is also well versed in administration and political affairs. Such a jurist is introduced as an expert on human psychology and who can take over the function of a leader and guardianship of Muslim affairs.

Master of affairs of Muslims also in administration of Islamic countries is having special powers of the Infallible Imams (a) and he uses his powers in administration of the country.

That is why an Islamic government under no circumstances, in emergency of shortage, applies necessary rules and regulations, because in order to solve political difficulties it either depends on jurisprudential derivations (*Ijtihaadaat*) of the jurists who are conversant with the current situation or uses its own special powers.

From that which is mentioned above, it is known that rules and regulations of Islam can be everlasting and assure the success of man in the world and the hereafter. That is why there is no doubt in the finality of prophethood of the Prophet of Islam.

Why the sending of legislative prophets ended?

It is possible that someone may raise other petty objections and say: since we have accepted that after the advent of the Prophet of Islam we do not have need of legislative prophets, we don't accept that there is no more need for missionary prophets also. The past prophets were of two types: some were owners of a separate Shariah (*Ulul Azm*) and there were some who only propagated the religion of these Ulul Azm prophets, which was very effective and beneficial in the guidance of people. After the Prophet of Islam also the existence of such prophets would have been definitely beneficial; thus why were they not continued?

In reply, it can be said that the sending of prophets is there to exhaust the argument under necessary circumstances. After the Prophet of Islam such a need did not exist any more, because man by that time had matured in practical and theoretical intellect and knowledge and thus he was now capable of guarding and propagating his religious and intellectual heritage. Hence at that time religion was perfected and became needless of a missionary.

Almighty Allah says in the Holy Quran:

ٱلۡيَوۡمَ يَئِسَ ٱلَّذِينَ كَفَرُواْ مِن دِينِكُمۡ فَلَا تَخۡشَوۡهُمۡ وَٱخۡشَوۡنِۚ ٱلۡيَوۡمَ أَكۡمَلۡتُ لَكُمۡ دِينَكُمۡ وَأَتۡمَمۡتُ عَلَيۡكُمۡ نِعۡمَتِي وَرَضِيتُ لَكُمُ ٱلۡإِسۡلَٰمَ دِينࣰا

"This day have those who disbelieve despaired of your religion, so fear them not, and fear Me. This day have I perfected for you your religion and completed My favor on you and chosen for you Islam as a religion..." (5:3)

Islam has given the responsibility of guarding and propagating faith to three groups of persons:

First: The Infallible Imam: Shia believe that after the Prophet of Islam (ṣ), the responsibility of guarding and propagating religion and administration of Islamic nation is entrusted to the Infallible Imam. During his lifetime, the Messenger of Allah (ṣ) appointed Imam Ali (a) for this purpose and entrusted to him the necessary information so that after him he may guard and promote the religion of Islam.

Amirul Momineen (a) also during his lifetime, fulfilled his duty and as far as possible tried to defend religion and lead the nation and at the time of his passing away appointed Imam Hasan (a) in his place and transferred the necessary information to him. After Imam Hasan (a), Imam Husain (a) succeeded to Imamate and in this way every Imam specified the next Imam. This continued till the time of Imam Hasan Askari (a) in 255 A.H.

As a result of the efforts and struggles of the Infallible Imams (a), hundreds of thousands of sayings regarding various subjects were bestowed to Muslims which remained for future generations and due to the efforts of the Holy Imams (a) thousands of intellectuals, Islamic scholars and missionaries were trained.

The Eleventh Imam also, at the time of his passing away, appointed his son, Hujjat Ibnul Hasan (a) as the Imam in his place and transferred to him the responsibility of protecting religion. The Twelfth Imam is in occultation from that time till the present day and he is fulfilling his duties in other ways, although every moment he is in anticipation of the day when people would be fully ready for his Islamic revolution and the rule of absolute justice and equity. At that time, he would spread Islam to all corners of the world with a universal revolution and fill the earth with justice and equity like it would have been filled with injustice and oppression.

From what is mentioned above, it can be concluded that by the legislation of the post of Imamate, there is no need of sending missionary prophets who may propagate Islam, because this responsibility is given over to the Infallible Imams.

Second: Jurists and scholars of religion: During the period of Infallibles (a) many intellectuals and scholars acquired knowledge of Islamic laws and sciences and became ready to propagate them. The Prophet of Islam (s) and Holy Imams (a) made great efforts to nurture such persons.

Regarding this, we have a large number of traditions and some of them are mentioned below:

Imam Ja'far Sadiq (a) said:

> *Scholars are the heirs of the prophets. Prophets do not leave behind any material wealth; on the contrary, they leave traditions in inheritance. Thus anyone who takes something from those traditions earns a great advantage. Take care from whom you obtain your knowledge. Among us Ahl al-Bayt (a) in every generation there exist just persons who refrain from distortion of the extremists, deviation of the misguided and interpretation of the ignorant.*[1]

---

[1] *Al-Kafi*, Vol. 1, Pg. 32

The Messenger of Allah (ṣ) said:

The scholars of my Ummah are like the prophets of Bani Israel.[1]

In the same way, he said:

May Allah have mercy on my successors. He was asked: O Messenger of Allah (ṣ), who are your successors? He replied: One who revives my practice and reminds people about it.[2]

He also said:

The simile of the scholars on the earth is the simile of the stars on the sky as people seek directions through them in darkness in land and seas and if they disappear it is feared that those who are guided by them would be lost.[3]

Amirul Momineen (a) has narrated from the Messenger of Allah (ṣ) that he said:

On Judgment Day, the ink of the scholars will weighed against the blood of martyrs and the ink of the scholars will be found to be superior to the blood of martyrs.[4]

The Messenger of Allah (ṣ) said:

For one who dies while being in pursuit of knowledge aimed at revival of Islam, there is only a difference of one stage between him and the prophets.[5]

---

[1] *Biharul Anwar*, Vol. 2, Pg. 21
[2] *Biharul Anwar*, Vol. 2, Pg. 25
[3] *Biharul Anwar*, Vol. 2, Pg. 25
[4] *Biharul Anwar*, Vol. 2, Pg. 16
[5] *Biharul Anwar*, Vol. 1, Pg. 184

It can be concluded from these and similar traditions that the Holy Prophet (ṣ) has placed the responsibility of guiding the people upon the religious scholars. In such a case there is no need of sending missionary prophets.

Third: Human Intellect: One of the important aims of the prophets was nurturing and perfection of intellects. The past prophets played a very important role in this regard. Human intellects were gradually perfected through the ages through the efforts of prophets till they reached absolute maturity during the time of the Prophet of Islam (ṣ). The Prophet of Islam (ṣ) also had a special quality with regard to development and perfection of human intellect. He advised people that they should use their intellects and be inquisitive to discover realities and understand facts and that they should discriminate between truth and falsehood through contemplation and should only accept the truth.

In numerous verses, the Holy Quran had encouraged people to use intellect and contemplation. In books of traditions also there are a large number of traditions that praise intelligence and advise people to gain knowledge and intelligence. The Prophet of Islam (ṣ) and the Holy Imams (a) have mentioned the intellect to be a guide and a religious evidence in identification of intellectual subjects and problems and have asked them to use their intellect to identify the realities and to follow them.

It can thus be concluded that after the advent of the Prophet of Islam (ṣ) there is no need of sending missionary prophets and that is why we can say that Prophet of Islam (ṣ) is the seal of the prophets and that prophethood has ended with him.

PROPHET MUHAMMAD (Ṣ) BEFORE BEING CONFERRED THE OFFICE OF PROPHETHOOD

The Holy Prophet Muhammad (ṣ) was born on 17th Rabiul Awwal in the year 570 A.D. in Mecca.[1]

His father was Abdullah and mother, Amina. His father passed away before his birth and was buried in Medina. The Prophet came under the care of his grandfather, Abdul Muttalib. Abdul Muttalib was a Quraish elder and was very fond of Muhammad. Regarding him, he said: My son, Muhammad is having a bright future.[2]

At the age of five years The Holy Prophet Muhammad (ṣ) also lost his mother, Amina and when he was hardly nine his grandfather, Abdul Muttalib also departed for his heavenly abode. After the passing away of Abdul Muttalib, his son, Abu Talib took over the responsibility of his upbringing and care. This kind uncle cared for Muhammad like a real father.

The Holy Prophet Muhammad, at the age of twenty-five years married Khadija bint Khuwaylid, a noble and chaste lady of Quraish. She gave birth to two sons, but

---

[1] Will Durant, *History of Civilization*, Part I, Vol. 4, Pg. 197
[2] *Manaqib Ibne Shahr Ashob*, Vol. 1, Pg. 61

they passed away a short time after birth. She also had four daughters named: Zaynab, Ruqayyah, Ummu Kulthum and Fatima.

It is learnt from history that The Holy Prophet Muhammad (ṣ) during his childhood and youth was better than others of his age and it was realized that he had an extraordinary personality.

Abu Talib says the following with regard to him:

When a part of the night had passed, I heard amazing statements from Muhammad (ṣ). He mentioned the name of God when he drank water or ate his dinner. When he began eating, I heard from Muhammad: In the name of Allah, the One. After eating, he remarked: Praise be to Allah in excess. I was amazed at these acts. Sometimes, I came upon him suddenly and saw effulgence over his head which continued up to the heavens. I never heard any falsehood from Muhammad and he never committed any act of the age of Ignorance. I never saw him laughing for no reason or playing with children; he was never attracted to them. He liked solitude and humility.[1]

Ibn Abbas says: In the morning, when the sons of Abu Talib awoke from sleep their eyes used to be dirty and sticky, but the eyes of Muhammad used to be absolutely clean. In the morning, Abu Talib provided breakfast to the children; they attacked the food competing with each other but Muhammad did not take part in this. When Abu Talib noticed this, he gave him food separately.[2]

---

[1] *Manaqib Ibne Shahr Ashob*, Vol. 1, Pg. 63
[2] Abul Fida, *Seerat Nabuwwa*, Vol. 1, Pg. 242

Abul Fida writes:

The Messenger of Allah (ṣ) grew up under the care of Abu Talib. Almighty Allah guarded him from committing the acts of the period of Ignorance and other evil deeds, because He wanted to exalt his status so that he may come out as the most excellent among his relatives with regard to greatness, good nature, observance of manners of society, kindness to neighbors, forbearance, trustworthiness and truthfulness. He never committed any vile deed and did not cause harm to anyone. He never entered into arguments and fights. All the praiseworthy qualities had gathered in him in such a way that he was given the title of 'Muhammad Amin'.[1]

Abul Fida writes:

In the beginning of revelation, the Holy Prophet (ṣ) returned home terrified and told his wife, Khadija: I am fearful about my own self. Khadija comforted him saying: Glad tidings be to you that Almighty Allah will not degrade you in any way. Because you are good to relatives; you are truthful and share the difficulties of people; you help the poor and are hospitable and you assist others in worldly matters.[2]

Anas ibn Malik says:

Before prophethood, The Holy Prophet Muhammad (ṣ) earned the title of Trustworthy (*Amin*) among the people as people had recognized his honesty and justice.

---

[1] Abul Fida, *Seerat Nabuwwa*, Vol. 1, Pg. 249

[2] Abul Fida, *Seerat Nabuwwa*, Vol. 1, Pg. 394

Rabi ibn Khaitham says: During the period of Ignorance, people used to refer to The Holy Prophet Muhammad (ṣ) in their disputes. Nadhr ibn Harith told Quraish: When Muhammad (ṣ) was a child you considered him better than you with regard to truthfulness and honesty, but when he has matured and is sent to you as the prophet of God, you allege that he is a sorcerer. No, by Allah, he is not a magician.[1]

The Holy Prophet Muhammad (ṣ) was twenty years of age when he took part in *Hilful Fuzool* – that is the oath of the valiant. Some well intending Arab gentlemen had devised this committee to protect the rights of oppressed and this was finalized at the house of Abdullah ibn Judan. They took oath that as long as they were alive, they would protect those who were oppressed and recover their rights from the usurpers. The Holy Prophet Muhammad (ṣ) said with regard to this:

I was present at the oath, which was taken in the house of Abdullah ibn Judan; and I would not like to be given red-haired camels in exchange for it; and even though Islam is established, if I am still called to it, I would respond.[2]

From such historical evidences, it can be concluded that The Holy Prophet Muhammad (ṣ), before declaration of prophethood was well known for his nice behavior, honesty, truthfulness, forbearance, justice, harmlessness and chastity.

As a result of this same fine behavior, people accepted his claim of prophethood and brought faith upon him.

---

[1] *Uyunul Athar*, Vol. 2, Pg. 334

[2] Abul Fida, *Seerat Nabuwwa*, Vol. 1, Pg. 257-262

Religion of Muhammad (ṣ) before being vested with the office of prophethood

The question which arises at this juncture is that whether The Holy Prophet Muhammad (ṣ) believed in religion and Shariah before being vested with the office of prophethood? And if he had faith; which religion did he follow?

Before that it is necessary to mention that regretfully we don't have anything in history and Islamic sources which can clearly oppose this matter, but it is possible to mention some points as historical evidences. For example, Abul Fida writes:

It was the practice of the Messenger of Allah (ṣ) that one month every year he used to go the Cave of Hira and engage in worship there. Quraish also performed this act during the period of Ignorance. They gave food to every mendicant who came to their town. After the worship rituals, before entering his house, he used to circumambulate the Kaaba.[1]

Ghyath ibn Ibrahim has narrated from Imam Ja'far Sadiq (a) that he said:

The Holy Prophet, after coming to Medina performed the Hajj only once. But he performed the Hajj rituals in Mecca along with his relatives a number of times.[2]

It is also mentioned that Muhammad (ṣ) prayed the ritual prayer at the age of four years.[3]

---

[1] Abul Fida, *Seerat Nabuwwa*, Vol. 1, Pg. 390
[2] *Wasailush Shia*, Vol. 8, Pg. 88
[3] *Biharul Anwar*, Vol. 15, Pg. 361

His uncle, Abu Talib also described the childhood of Muhammad in the same way: He recited 'In the name of Allah', before dinner and uttered 'praise be to Allah' after it.[1]

From such descriptions that are mentioned about His Eminence, it can be concluded that before being vested with the office of prophethood, he used to perform worship rituals, perform the ritual prayer and spend a month every year at the cave of Hira; he performed the rituals of Hajj, circumambulated the Kaaba and recited 'In the name of Allah' before eating; thus it can be seen that he was a religious person, who observed worship rituals diligently.

Moreover, in the discussion of infallibility, it was proved that prophets are immune from infidelity, polytheism and sins, throughout their lives. Hence it should be said that the Prophet of Islam also before his being vested with the office of prophethood was religious, because infidelity and polytheism are not compatible with his infallibility.

Quran has also absolutely negated deviation and infidelity for the Holy Prophet (s) even before he was vested with the office of prophethood. It even says:

وَٱلنَّجْمِ إِذَا هَوَىٰ ۝ مَا ضَلَّ صَاحِبُكُمْ وَمَا غَوَىٰ ۝

"I swear by the star when it goes down. Your companion does not err, nor does he go astray..." (53:1-2)

Therefore there cannot be doubt about the religiosity of Muhammad before his being vested with the office of prophethood.

---

[1] *Manaqib Ibne Shahr Ashob*, Vol. 1, Pg. 63

After accepting his original religiosity now the question arises that which religion was he following? Here a number of possibilities exist:

First possibility: He either followed the Shariah of Prophet Musa or Prophet Isa (a), since only these two heavenly religions existed in the world and it was necessary for all to follow them. Thus Prophet Muhammad (s) also before being vested with prophethood must have followed one of these faiths.

But this possibility is invalid; because if he had been a Jew or a Christian he would also have taken part in the rituals of their faith and would have socialized with them; and this would have been recorded in history; whereas such a thing is neither recorded in history nor the Jews and Christians have claimed this.

Thus as you know from before, The Holy Prophet Muhammad believed in rituals and worships which are from other than these two religions; like Hajj, circumambulating the Kaaba, ritual prayer and Etekaf (seclusion) in the Cave of Hira. On the basis of this, it can be concluded that he was neither a Jew nor a Christian before his being vested with prophethood.

Second possibility: That he was a follower of the Shariah of Prophet Ibrahim (a). In explanation of this point, it can be said that Prophet Ibrahim (a) laid the foundation of monotheism and God worship in Hijaz. His Shariah became famous in that area as Hanifiyya and it spread among the people there. His son, Ismail also propagated that Shariah. Arabs of that area, who were most probably descendants of Prophet Ismail (a) accepted the Shariah of their ancestor, Prophet Ibrahim (a) and they preserved it.

For a long time, the religion of Prophet Ibrahim (a) was the predominant religion of the people of Arabian Peninsula, but due to the passage of time, laws, rules and worship rituals of that Hanif faith were gradually forgotten and neglected and except for some special rituals like Hajj, stay at Arafat, Mashar and Mina, animal sacrifice, stoning of satans, circling the Kaaba, trotting between Safa and Marwa and some other rituals. On the contrary, by the passage of time polytheism dominated the beliefs of the people and through wrong justification they considered some things and persons as associates of God, and worshipped them. In spite of these deviations, they considered themselves as the followers of the religion of Ibrahim (a).

Although there were some among them who were displeased with the present situation and they realized the loss of the essence of the religion of Ibrahim (a) and of having fallen into deviation and sometimes they even went so far as to adopt the laws and customs of religious worship of the upright faith and purify them from nonsense. The following historical examples prove this point:

Ibn Hisham writes:

On one of the festivals, when Quraish used to gather around an idol and with absolute sincerity offer sacrifice to it four persons separated from them, receded into a corner and spoke among themselves: We take oath that we would keep our faith concealed from others. Those four were as follows: Waraqa ibn Naufal, Abdullah ibn Jahash, Uthman ibn Huwairath and Zaid ibn Umar. They said: By Allah, you know that your people do not follow the right faith. They have adopted the wrong version of the faith of your ancestor, Ibrahim (a). What is the stone that they go around? This idol neither hears nor sees, nor causes any harm or benefit. My people! Select the right faith for yourself. After that they dispersed in the land to revive the religion of Ibrahim (a).[1]

He also writes:

Zaid ibn Umar waited; came out of the religion of his relatives but he did not join the religion of Jews and Christians. He kept away from idol worship, abstained from carrion, blood and animals sacrificed to the idols. He prohibited the killing of the child and said: I worship only the God of Ibrahim (a). Thus he condemned the religion of his people.[2]

It can be concluded from such reports that the ancestors of the Prophet also followed the religion of Ibrahim (a).

Asbagh ibn Nubatah says that he heard Amirul Momineen (a) say:

By Allah, the father and grandfather of Abu Talib, and Hashim and Abd Manaf never worshipped idols. He was asked: Then how did they worship? He replied: They acted on the religion of Ibrahim (a) and prayed facing the Holy Kaaba.[3]

On the basis of this, it can be realized that The Holy Prophet Muhammad (s) followed the religion and Shariah of Ibrahim (a) before his prophethood. He was a

---

[1] Ibne Hisham, *Seerat Nabawiyya*, Vol. 1, Pg. 237

[2] Ibne Hisham, *Seerat Nabawiyya*, Vol. 1, Pg. 239

[3] *Biharul Anwar*, Vol. 15, Pg. 144

monotheist and he opposed polytheism and idol worship. He prayed the ritual prayer and performed the rituals of Hajj, which are in fact the rituals of the religion of Ibrahim (a). He was fond of seclusion and remembrance of God and observed good manners and morals.

It can be concluded from some traditional reports that The Holy Prophet Muhammad (s), even before his ministry, was always having divine help in recognizing the best morals and its demands.

Amirul Momineen (a) says with regard to this:

From the time of his weaning, Allah had put a mighty angel with him to take him along the path of high character and good behavior through day and night.[1]

Allamah Majlisi has written with regard to this:

It is narrated that some companions of Imam Muhammad Baqir (a) asked him about the interpretation of the verse:

إِلَّا مَنِ ارْتَضَىٰ مِن رَّسُولٍ فَإِنَّهُ يَسْلُكُ مِنْ بَيْنِ يَدَيْهِ وَمِنْ خَلْفِهِ رَصَدًا ۝

"Except to him whom He chooses as an apostle; for surely He makes a guard to march before him and after him." (72:27)

The Imam said:

Almighty Allah appoints angels on his prophets to guard them and help them in propagating their message. He appointed a mighty angel since the time of Muhammad's infancy, to guard him and to guide him to good deeds and praiseworthy morals and to restrain him from evil. It was this angel who said:

---

[1] *Nahjul Balagha*, Sermon 194

Peace be on you, O Muhammad, Messenger of Allah (ṣ) when he was not even given the ministry, the Prophet thought that this salutation was from stones and the earth; but no matter how much he searched, he could not find anything.[1]

---

[1] *Biharul Anwar*, Vol. 15, Pg. 361

MINISTRY OF THE HOLY PROPHET

The Holy Prophet Muhammad (s) was appointed as a prophet on 27th Rajab in the year 610 A.D. at the age of forty years.[1] It is mentioned in history that before his appointment also, he often used to see signs in his sleep and wakefulness; he saw Jibraeel and heard his voice; so much so that he sometimes addressed him as the Messenger of Allah (s).

Bulazari writes:

When Almighty Allah wanted to exalt the status of Muhammad (s) and to begin his prophethood, it so happened that he came out of the town to answer the call of nature and retired into the passes and caves and he did not pass a single tree, but that it greeted him saying: Peace be on you, O Messenger of Allah (s). Thus His Eminence looked here and there but could see no one.[2]

Sometimes during sleep and wakefulness, he used to see a person who said to him: Peace be on you, O Messenger of Allah (s). He asked him: Who are you? He replied: I am Jibraeel. Allah has sent me so that I may select you for prophethood. The Messenger of Allah (s) witnessed such incidents, but he did not speak about them to anyone.[3]

---

[1] *Biharul Anwar*, Vol. 18, Pg. 189
[2] *Ansabul Ashraf*, Vol. 1, Pg. 104
[3] *Biharul Anwar*, Vol. 18, Pg. 184

Sometimes he mentioned the matter to his wife, Khadija and she told him that she was hopeful that it would be as such.[1]

Bulazari writes:

The first stage of revelation was a true dream. He never dreamed except that it was clear to him like daylight. Thus he became inclined to seclusion and retired to Hira Cave and remained there in seclusion, worshipping his God. He stayed there in Etekaf for some nights. After that he came back to Khadija and continued to lead his family life. Till the time that in the Cave of Hira, he realized the truth and Jibraeel spoke to him.[2]

The life history of the Messenger of Allah (ṣ) was such that every year for a period of at least one month, he remained in the cave of Hira engrossed in worship.[3]

Ubaid ibn Umair says:

The Messenger of Allah (ṣ) retired to the cave of Hira for a month every year and remained there engrossed in worship. During those days he fed the poor. When the period of his stay was over he returned to Mecca and before entering his house circled the Kaaba seven or more times.[4]

Hira is a tall mountain to the north of Mecca having elevations towards Mina. Previously it was at a distance of one Farsakh from the city, but today the city has

---

[1] *Biharul Anwar*, Vol. 18, Pg. 194
[2] *Ansabul Ashraf*, Vol. 1, Pg. 105
[3] *Seerat Ibne Hisham*, Vol. 1, Pg. 251
[4] *Seerat Ibne Hisham*, Vol. 1, Pg. 252

expanded to reach within the vicinity of this mountain. At the center of this mountain there is a cave having the capacity to house three persons and this cave is called as the Cave of Hira. It is the place of Etekaf and worship of Prophet Muhammad (ṣ) and the location of the descent of the angel of revelation. For months he remained in sincere worship in this illuminated cave and day and night was engrossed in the worship of the Lord of the worlds and spoke confidentially to Him.

He sat on a rocky platform and spent hours in religious contemplation and pondered on the amazing aspects of creation. He was amazed at the stars that filled the beautiful sky of Mecca. He witnessed the beautiful sunrise and sunset for this same place. He pondered on the amazing aspects of human body, trees, vegetations, animals, mountains and plains, oceans and the turbulent waves and prostrated before the greatness and might of the God creator of the universe.

Sometimes he felt sorry for the ignorance of people in leaving the creator of the world and taking up the worship of idols having no specialty.

At other times he thought about the oppression of nobles and rich and oppression of the deprived and troubles and he searched for its solution. When he was aggrieved from all sides, he turned to Almighty Allah and spoke to Him from the depths of his heart and sought His help in solving the religious and social problems of man.

When the month of Etekaf came to an end, he returned to Mecca with a satisfied and illuminated heart and a heart filled with contentment and hope and after circling the Kaaba went home and continues living a normal life.

The life of the Prophet of Islam till the age of forty passed in this way and after that came the time of his ministry.

When the Messenger of Allah (ṣ) was forty years of age, as per his habit, he retired to the Cave of Hira for contemplation and worship. This year he chose the month of Rajab for Etekaf. Contemplation and worship of His Eminence, in this year was more and deeper than that of the previous years. He prolonged his prostrations further and adopted more sincerity in speaking to Almighty Allah directly; similarly his contemplation was also deeper as if he was having completely different surroundings. His religious emotion was charged and his being had become illuminated with effulgence of his future ministry pulling him towards the heights of ethereal luminosity.

Days and nights of Rajab passed in this way and along with it more intense spiritual emotions overtook him and the soul of Prophet Muhammad (ṣ) became more and more prepared to establish a connection with the unseen world and to receive divine revelations.

The 27th of Rajab arrived and The Holy Prophet Muhammad (ṣ) was immersed in contemplation, when Jibraeel came down and announced: You are the Messenger of Allah and you have been appointed to convey the message of God.[1]

---

[1] Story of the beginning of ministry and the first time Jibraeel came down is mentioned in books of history in different ways. Some of them do not befit the position of prophethood. That is why in reporting this extraordinary incident we have relied only on traditions of Ahle Bayt (a.s.) as they were more knowledgeable than others.

Imam Hadi (a) has recounted the incident of revelation as follows:

When the Messenger of Allah (ṣ) returned from trade in Syria he distributed all that he had earned on the way among the poor and needy. He went to the cave of Hira everyday and climbed its summit and saw the signs of divine mercy and amazing wisdom of God. He looked at the earth and the sky, the seas and wilderness and gained lessons from them. He worshipped Almighty Allah as He deserves to be worshipped.

When he reached the age of forty, Almighty Allah made his heart as the best and most obedient and humble of all the hearts; thus the doors of heavens opened for him so that he may see them. He permitted the angels to descend and Muhammad (ṣ) looked at them. He sent down His mercy and it surrounded everything from the Throne to the head of Muhammad. He saw Jibraeel (the trustworthy spirit) come down to him in a halo of light. Jibraeel held the arm of the Prophet and pressed it saying: O Muhammad, read. He asked: What should I read? Jibraeel said: O Muhammad,

اقْرَأْ بِاسْمِ رَبِّكَ الَّذِي خَلَقَ ۝ خَلَقَ الْإِنسَانَ مِنْ عَلَقٍ ۝ اقْرَأْ وَرَبُّكَ الْأَكْرَمُ ۝ الَّذِي عَلَّمَ بِالْقَلَمِ ۝ عَلَّمَ الْإِنسَانَ مَا لَمْ يَعْلَمْ ۝

"Read in the name of your Lord Who created. He created man from a clot. Read and your Lord is Most Honorable, Who taught (to write) with the pen Taught man what he knew not." (96:1-5)

At that moment Jibraeel revealed to Muhammad (ṣ) what he had brought from Almighty Allah and returned to the heavens.

Muhammad (s) came down from Mount Hira while as a result of witnessing the majesty of God he was in a trance-like condition. Seeing Jibraeel and bearing the divine revelation weighed so much on Muhammad (s) that he shook like a feverish person. He was in fact fearful of the fact that Quraish would refute him and allege that he was insane. Whereas the truth was that he was the most sensible and the most honored of the people there. He was absolutely aloof of the Satan and the words and deeds of insane persons.

Thus Almighty Allah intended to expand his breast and give peace to him. Therefore the mountains, rocks, pebbles on which he walked, all saluted him and said: Peace be on you, O Muhammad, Peace be on you, O the saint of Allah, Peace be on you, O Messenger of Allah (s). Glad tidings be to you that God has given you excellence and elegance and exalted you over all the past and future men. Do not be aggrieved that Quraish would label you as a madman, because one who is given excellence by Allah is the one who is excellent in the real sense and one whom Allah has made noble is the one who is noble in the real sense. Do not be discouraged by the condemnation of Quraish and evil among the Arabs, Allah would soon convey you to the loftiest position and the most honored rank.[1]

On seeing Jibraeel and on receiving revelation, the complete being of The Holy Prophet Muhammad (s) became illuminated by a powerful faith and a confident conscience and he returned home from mount Hira.

---

[1] *Biharul Anwar*, Vol. 18, Pg. 205

Ibn Shahr Ashob writes:

Muhammad (s) came home and the house was illuminated with his effulgence. His wife, Khadija was amazed and she asked: What effulgence is this? The Holy Prophet (s) replied: It is the effulgence of prophethood. Say: I testify that there is no god, except Allah; Muhammad is the messenger of Allah. Khadija asked: I have been aware of this since a long time and she embraced Islam at that time.[1]

There is difference of opinion among scholars with regard to the matter that which was the first chapter to be revealed on the Messenger of Allah (s). Most historians consider Surah Alaq to be the first in this regard and the same point is mentioned in some traditions.

Ali ibn Sirri has narrated from Imam Ja'far Sadiq (a) that he said:

The first chapter to be revealed on the Messenger of Allah (s) was this:

$$\text{... بِسْمِ اللهِ الرَّحْمَنِ الرَّحِيمِ اقْرَأْ بِاسْمِ رَبِّكَ}$$

"In the name of Allah, the Beneficent, the Merciful. Read in the name of your Lord..." (96:1)

And the last chapter was:

$$\text{... إِذَا جَاءَ نَصْرُ اللهِ}$$

"When there comes the help of Allah..." (110:1)[2]

---

[1] *Manaqib Aale Abi Talib*, Vol. 1, Pg. 72
[2] *Al-Kafi*, Vol. 2, Pg. 628

REVELATION AND PRESERVATION OF QURAN

Quran is a heavenly book and the word of God Almighty. Lofty matters and facts of Quran have come down in the form of Arabic words and sentences which were sent down to the illuminated heart of the Prophet of Islam through Jibraeel.

Verses of Quran were revealed on the Prophet of Islam in a period of 23 years on different appropriate occasions in journey and at home and in war as well as peace.

Sometimes one verse, sometimes a number of verse and at other times even a whole chapter was revealed at a time.

The Holy Quran has 114 chapters and all of them except Surah Taubah begin with the formula: In the name of Allah, the Beneficent, the Merciful. Every chapter is composed of a number of verses. The big chapters are called as the long chapters and the small chapters are called as the short chapters.

A number of chapters were revealed in Mecca or its surroundings and they are known as the Meccan chapters and others were revealed in Medina and its surroundings and they are Medinan chapters.

The Holy Prophet (s) paid special attention in order to preserve the collection of Quran and to prevent it from interpolation and alteration, and that is why he performed the following three actions:

1. Whenever a verse was revealed on the illuminated heart of the Prophet, he recited it immediately and stored it in his memory, never forgetting it, because his infallibility prevented him from forgetting it or making a mistake in it.

Quran says:

"We will make you recite so you shall not forget..." (87:6)

The Holy Prophet (s) paid attention to recitation of Quran and its repetition and he recited it on every appropriate occasion. He quoted the relevant verses in sermons, explanation of Islamic laws and moral topics. He recited parts of Quran in obligatory and recommended ritual prayers. Everyday he recited a number of verses and especially during the days of Ramadan. Although the Holy Prophet (s) had never attended a school he knew the whole Quran by heart and he recited it in the sequence of its revelation. He was infallible and immune from mistakes in receiving it from Jibraeel, its preservation and its conveyance.

2. The Holy Prophet (s) recited to the companions every chapter or verse that was revealed on him and also encouraged them to learn them by heart, and Muslims also made efforts to listen to the revealed verses and to commit them to memory. The Holy Prophet (s) also in

this regard tried that the verses that people learnt should be correct and without any error. Memorizers of Quran also recited the verses of Quran in presence of the Holy Prophet (ṣ) in order to make sure of their accuracy.

Through this method, a large number of companions learnt the correct recitation of Quran and among them seven persons became famed in this regard.

Suyuti writes: Among those who recited the Quran in the presence of the Holy Prophet (ṣ), seven became more famed; they were: Uthman, Ali, Ubayy, Zaid ibn Thabit, Ibn Masud, Abul Darda and Abu Musa Ashari.[1]

Since the Messenger of Allah (ṣ) laid so much emphasis on memorizing the Quran, a large number of companions according to their capacities, memorized at least a part of it. Among them some of them succeeded in learning it by heart; and they were named as 'reciters' (*Qurra*) or 'memorizers of Quran' (*Hafiz Quran*). Their exact number is not known, but they were considerable in number.

Suyuti has narrated from Qurtubi that he said: Seventy reciters of Quran (*Qurra*) were killed in the Battle of Yamama. During the time of the Holy Prophet (ṣ) the same number were killed at the well of Maoona.[2]

From this statement it can be concluded that the memorizers of Quran were in such large numbers that 140 persons were killed only in these two battles. Although it is not known that those who were killed knew the whole Quran by heart or only a part of it.

---

[1] *Al-Itqan fee Uloomul Quran*, Vol. 1, Pg. 96
[2] *Al-Itqan fee Uloomul Quran*, Vol. 1, Pg. 94

Some writers believe that those who knew the whole Quran by heart were less than this number.

Shaykh Abdul Hayy Qattani writes:

During the time of the Holy Prophet (s) ten persons knew the whole Quran by heart: Ali, Uthman, Ubayy ibn Kaab, Maaz ibn Jabal. Abul Darda, Zaid ibn Thabit, Abu Zaid Ansari, Tamim Dari, Ubadah ibn Thabit and Abu Ayyub.[1]

3. Transcription and compilation. The Messenger of Allah (s) chose some persons to transcribe the Quran. When a verse or some verses were revealed, he summoned one of them and dictated the same and they put it in writing. After that he asked the scribe to read what he has written. He listened carefully and if there was even the slightest mistake, he corrected it. Sometimes the Holy Prophet (s) used to specify the place where the scribe was supposed to record the verse and for example say: Write down this verse in such and such chapter after such and such verse.[2]

The Messenger of Allah (s) had a large number of scribes and they are said to be up to 43 persons.[3] But all of them were not scribes of revelation; on the contrary some were scribes who wrote the letters of His Eminence.

Shaykh Abdul Hayy writes: Uthman ibn Affan and Ali were the scribes of revelation, when these two persons were not present, Ubayy ibn Kaab and Zaid ibn Thabit were entrusted with the duty. If none of them were

---

[1] *Al-Tarateeb al-Idariya*, Vol. 1, Pg. 46

[2] *Tarikh Yaqubi*, Vol. 2, Pg. 43

[3] *Al-Tarateeb al-Idariya*, Vol. 1, Pg. 115-116

present, any other scribe that was present there was given the job. They were as follows: Muawiyah, Jabir ibn Saeed, Aban ibn Saeed, Alaa Hadhrami, Hanzala ibn Rabi.[1] These were of those who wrote a special copy of Quran for the Messenger of Allah (s). Although there were others also who recorded the verses in their private copies, so much so that some scribes of revelation in addition to the copy of the Holy Prophet (s) used to make a copy for themselves.

Writers began every chapter with the formula: In the name of Allah, the Beneficent, the Merciful, which was revealed at the beginning of every chapter. They continued to add verses to it till a new 'In the name of Allah, the Beneficent, the Merciful' was revealed, which was a sign that it was a new chapter. After that they transcribed new verses, except in special cases when the Messenger of Allah (s) ordered that such and such verse should be placed in some other chapter in a particular place.

Yaqubi writes:

Ibn Abbas says: When we saw 'In the name of Allah, the Beneficent, the Merciful' we understood that the previous chapter was over and a new chapter was beginning.[2]

Paper of that time

There is no doubt that the scribes of revelation inscribed the verses of Quran on things, therefore it is remarkable that we should know what type of paper existed at that

---

[1] *Al-Tarateeb al-Idariya,* Vol. 1, Pg. 114

[2] *Tarikh Yaqubi,* Vol. 2, Pg. 34

time. It is learnt from Quran that during the time of the Prophet of Islam, a thing existed, which was named as Qirtas.

The Holy Quran says:

$$وَلَوْ نَزَّلْنَا عَلَيْكَ كِتَٰبًا فِى قِرْطَاسٍ فَلَمَسُوهُ بِأَيْدِيهِمْ لَقَالَ ٱلَّذِينَ كَفَرُوٓا۟ إِنْ هَٰذَآ إِلَّا سِحْرٌ مُّبِينٌ ۝$$

"And if We had sent to you a writing on a paper, then they had touched it with their hands, certainly those who disbelieve would have said: This is nothing but clear enchantment." (6:7)

We learn from history that paper was already in existence during the time of the Prophet. In China it was manufactured from grass. In India, they wrote on pieces of white silk. In Iran they wrote on thin tanned leather, which was called *Adeem*. White and thin slabs of stone, copper sheets, iron and zinc, and barks of date trees, shoulder bone of the camel and goat; pieces of wood were all used as writing surfaces.[1]

Scribes of revelation wrote down the verses of Quran on the above mentioned objects and handed them over to the Holy Prophet (ṣ). His Eminence stored them in a special place in his house so that at the time of his passing away, a complete copy of Quran would be available with him.

Probably at the time of his passing away, the Prophet of Islam entrusted this same copy to Imam Ali (a), who was himself a scribe of revelation.

---

[1] *Al-Tarateeb al-Idariya*, Vol. 1, Pg. 122; Suyuti, *Al-Itqan*, Vol. 1, Pg. 78

Imam Ja'far Sadiq (a) says:

The Messenger of Allah (ṣ) said to Imam Ali (a): O Ali, Quran is placed behind my bed and it is written on a scroll, silk and papers. So take it and do not lose it like the Jews who allowed the Taurat to be lost.[1]

Compilation of Quran

As mentioned previously, verses of Quran were revealed disparately on the Messenger of Allah (ṣ) during a period of 23 years and he paid special attention to have them compiled and recorded. It was compiled a number of times till it came into the hands of Muslims in the present form:

First instance: During the lifetime of the Holy Prophet

The first step that the Prophet of Islam took was that he ordered the transcription of the revealed verses on sheets. He himself supervised the transcription and specified the proper place where a particular verse was supposed to be written. He separated the chapters and gave a title to each of them. He asked the scribes to read what they had written so that it may be free of errors. Then he took the sheets and stored them in a safe place. In this way, all the verses and chapters of Quran were gathered with His Eminence, but it is not known in what sequence were they placed and whether they were in some special sequence as followed in the recording of chapters?

It can be concluded from some statements that the method of compilation and arrangement was finalized

---

[1] *Biharul Anwar,* Vol. 92, Pg. 48

during the lifetime of the Holy Prophet (s) and under his supervision.

Zaid ibn Thabit says:

We were employed with the Messenger of Allah (s) to compile Quran from pages.[1]

It is not known correctly that how this new compilation was and how it was completed.

Collection and compilation of Quran at that time was not restricted to the copies of the Holy Prophet (s); on the contrary a number of scribes of revelation also wrote down the verses for themselves and in this way other copies of Quran also came into being, which is mentioned in books of traditions, exegesis and history. Like the copy of Ali (a), copy of Ibn Masud, copy of Ubayy Ibn Kaab and the copy of Zaid.

Ibn Nadeem has introduced them as follows: Those who compiled the Quran during the lifetime of the Prophet are as follows: Ali Ibn Abi Talib (a), Saad ibn Ubaid, Abul Darda, Uwaim ibn Zaid, Maaz ibn Jabal, Abu Zaid, Thabit ibn Zaid, Ubayy ibn Kaab, Ubaid ibn Muawiyah and Thabit ibn Zahhak.[2]

Each of them had a copy of Quran, which contained all the chapters and verses. But they had two defects: One was that they were not arranged in the shape of a book and secondly there was difference between them with regard to sequence of chapters.[3]

---

[1] Suyuti, *Al-Itqan,* Vol. 1, Pg. 76
[2] *Fehrist*, Pg. 47
[3] *Fehrist*, Pg. 43-48

The Messenger of Allah (ṣ) collected the verses and chapters of Quran in another way also: That is its preservation through the honest memorization of Quran, which took place as per the advice of the Prophet. A large number of people became engrossed in memorizing the Quran and some of them succeeded in learning the whole Quran by heart and they came to be called as those who knew the whole Quran by heart (*Hafizaan Quran*). They commanded great respect among companions and are considered to be protectors of Quran. Quran was transferred to others through memory. Muslims also referred to them when need arose. So much so that even the compilers of Quran during the time of Abu Bakr and Uthman also relied on them.

During the time of the Holy Prophet (ṣ), all the verses of Quran were gathered and compiled in this way and remained thus for the Muslims.

Second instance: During Abu Bakr's tenure

Although during the time of the Messenger of Allah (ṣ) and under his direct supervision, the compilation of all the verses and chapters of Quran was completed, in the same way a number of companions had also memorized it; but for more satisfaction another action was necessary; because firstly: Verses and chapters had not been compiled in one place in the form of a book. Instead it was on various scattered sheets and hence prone to alteration.

Secondly: Memorizers of Quran who were the protectors of this heavenly scripture who were referred to in times of need, were prone to death or martyrdom. It was feared that with their death, some verses would be lost. As happened during the Battle of Yamama that a number of memorizers of Quran were killed, till Abu Bakr realized this danger and issued the command that the whole of the Quran should be compiled into a book.

With regard to this, Suyuti writes: Zaid ibn Thabit said: Abu Bakr summoned me after the Battle of Yamama while Umar ibn Khattab was also present there. He said to me: Umar came to me and said: In the Battle of Yamama, a large number of reciters and memorizers of Quran are killed; I fear that in other battles also memorizers of Quran would be killed in this way and hence the Quran will be lost. In my view you should issue orders for the compilation of Quran.

Zaid says: I asked Umar: How can I do something that the Holy Prophet (s) did not do? Umar replied: By God, this is a good and a necessary job, and emphasized so much on it that I was also convinced. Zaid says: Abu Bakr said to me: You are an intelligent and trustworthy young man and you were a scribe of revelation; gather the Quran accurately and diligently. I gathered the Quran from the barks of date palms, bones of quadrupeds and white slabs of stone and from the memories of those who had learnt it by heart.[1]

Zaid ibn Thabit, as per the orders of Abu Bakr, accepted this important responsibility and became engrossed in it. He sought the help of companions of the Holy Prophet (s) also and said: Anyone who is in possession of a copy of Quran, or has memorized a chapter or some verses, should present it to me so that I may record it. Companions accepted his call and agreed to co-operate.

---

[1] Suyuti, *Al-Itqan fee Uloomul Quran*, Vol. 1, Pg. 76

Zaid fixed the testimony of two just persons as the criteria for acceptance of the verses. If two just men testified that they heard them from the Holy Prophet (s) or witnessed that it was written in the presence of the Holy Prophet (s), it was accorded acceptance and recorded.

Suyuti writes:

It is narrated from Laith ibn Saad that he said: Abu Bakr was the first to have the Quran compiled and he gave this responsibility to Zaid ibn Thabit. People presented the verses of Quran to Zaid but he didn't accept anything unless supported by the testimony of two just males.[1]

In the same way, he writes:

Umar said: All those who had taken something of Quran from the Holy Prophet (s) presented them so that it may be recorded. Companions had written the verses on paper, tablets, barks of date trees, but nothing was accepted except through the testimony of two just men.[2]

Although it should be mentioned that Zaid ibn Thabit was capable of this appointment from every aspect. Because firstly: he had faith, piety and was well known for trustworthiness and sagacity. Secondly: He was himself a memorizer of the Holy Quran and he had recited it before the Holy Prophet (s) twice and was certified as correct. Thirdly, he was a usual scribe of revelation. Fourthly: He was in possession of a copy of Quran which was certified by the Prophet.

---

[1] Suyuti, *Al-Itqan fee Uloomul Quran*, Vol. 1, Pg. 77

[2] Suyuti, *Al-Itqan fee Uloomul Quran*, Vol. 1, Pg. 77

Zaid ibn Thabit, who had such an excellence and being supported by all the other memorizers, after a diligent exercise, he compiled the Quran in a single copy and presented it to Abu Bakr. After Abu Bakr, this copy came into the charge of Umar and after him it was handed over to his daughter, Hafsa.

Compilation of Quran by Ali Ibn Abi Talib (a)

It can be concluded from some traditions and statements of some historians that Ali Ibn Abi Talib (a) was the first of those who after the passing away of the Messenger of Allah (s) became engrossed in compiling the Quran as per the orders of the Holy Prophet (s).

Abu Bakr Hadhrami has narrated from Imam Ja'far Sadiq (a) that the Messenger of Allah (s) said to Imam Ali (a):

> *Quran is placed behind my bed and it is written on scroll, paper and silk; take it and compile it and do not allow it to be lost like the Jews allowed Taurat to be lost. Thus Imam Ali (a) went out and gathered them in a yellow piece of cloth and placed a seal upon it in his house and remarked: I will not put the cloak on my shoulder (to leave the house) till I don't compile the Quran. If someone came to his house, he appeared without his cloak.*[1]

Abu Rafe writes that the Holy Prophet (s), in his last moments said to Imam Ali (a): O Ali, take this Book of Allah. Imam Ali (a) gathered it in a piece of cloth and took it to his house. When the Holy Prophet (s) passed away, Imam Ali (a) began to compile the Quran and arranged it in sequence of its revelation and he was absolutely capable of this.[2]

---

[1] *Biharul Anwar* Vol. 2, Pg. 48

[2] *Manaqib Ibne Shahr Ashob*, Vol. 2, Pg. 41

Abd Khair has narrated from Imam Ali (a) that he said:

> *When the Messenger of Allah (ṣ) passed away, I took an oath that I would not put the cloak on my shoulder before compiling the Quran; thus I did not put the cloak on my shoulder except after I had compiled the Quran.*[1]

Ibn Sirrin has narrated from Imam Ali (a) that he said:

> *When the Messenger of Allah (ṣ) passed away, I made an oath to Allah, that I would not put the cloak on my shoulder except for the Friday prayer, till I do not compile the Quran.*[2]

It is mentioned in *Tarikh Yaqubi*:

That Ali Ibn Abi Talib (a) compiled the Quran after the passing away of the Messenger of Allah (ṣ) and loaded it on a camel and came and said: This is the Quran and I have compiled it.[3]

All this shows that at the end of his lifetime, the Holy Prophet (ṣ) handed over a valuable copy of Quran to Imam Ali (a) and said: Compile the Quran in one place. Imam Ali (a), after the passing away of the Messenger of Allah (ṣ) and after completing his funeral rituals, started compile the Quran and finally presented it to the caliph regime, but it was not accepted.

It is not absolutely clear what difference the Quran of Imam Ali (a) had with the present Quran, but it can be briefly said that its difference is not with regard to

---

[1] *Manaqib Ibne Shahr Ashob*, Vol. 2, Pg. 41

[2] Suyuti, *Al-Itqan*, Vol. 1, Pg. 77

[3] *Tarikh Yaqubi*, Vol. 2, Pg. 135

number of verses or chapters or change in some chapters or verses. Because it is proved beyond any doubt that no kind of alteration and change has taken place in Quran. Rather the present Quran is same as that which was revealed on the Holy Prophet (ṣ).

That is why if it had any difference, it would have been with regard to the following:

1. Verses and chapters in the Quran of Imam Ali (a) were compiled in the sequence of their revelation.

2. In verses which were abrogated, the abrogated verse was placed before the abrogating one.

3. Verses were recorded according to recitation of Messenger of Allah (ṣ).

4. Most probably the commentary and interpretation that the Holy Prophet (ṣ) had given to the clear and ambiguous verses and the context of their revelation were noted in the margins of that Quran or on other pages.

At the conclusion, we consider it necessary to reiterate the point that according to Shia faith, the Quran present among the Muslims today is the same as revealed to the Holy Prophet (ṣ) and is protected from every kind of interpolation and alteration. Therefore, as per the commands of the Holy Imams (a), they act on this same Quran.

Third instance: During the Tenure of Uthman

Its cause is explained as follows: After the battles of Armenia and Azerbaijan, Huzaifah Ibn Yaman came to Uthman and informed him about the severe differences in recitation of Quran and said: O Chief of believers, before Muslims also become involved in differences that Jews and Christians have in their scriptures, do something and prevent differences from appearing in Quran.[1]

Although during the time of Abu Bakr a complete copy of the Quran had been prepared and compiled, he handed it over to Umar and later it came into the custody of his daughter, Hafsa. But this Quran was not given to the public. Instead, people continued referring to the copies that scribes of revelation had compiled during the time of the Holy Prophet (s) and these copies had become popular in Islamic areas.

Regrettably, the versions of Quran which had gained popularity were not same. They had differences with regard to two aspects: one was with regard to the sequence of verses and chapters and secondly with regard to mode of script. In this manner, different versions of Quran appeared and became popular in Islamic areas. Every group defended its own version and considered it superior to others.

When Huzaifah saw these differences among Muslims, he was highly concerned and he perceived danger for the future of Quran and Muslims and after his return, mentioned it to Uthman and asked him to find a solution. Uthman also became extremely worried and decided to remove these differences and unite all the Muslims on a single version of Quran.

---

[1] *Jamiul Usul*, Vol. 2, Pg. 503

With this aim, he invited Zaid ibn Thabit and consulted him; because he was an expert of Quran and had compiled it during the time of Abu Bakr. Therefore he asked him to exercise diligence and compile a copy of Quran. He handed over the Quran of Abu Bakr to Huzaifah. He also ordered Abdullah ibn Zubair, Saeed ibn Aas, Abdur Rahman ibn Harith to cooperate with Huzaifah in this matter. After that, he said: Study the Quran closely and try to pronounce the letters and words correctly. So that when you notice a difference, you should give preference to the pronunciation of Quraish as Quran was revealed in the language of Quraish.[1]

This committee was formed in 25 A.H. at the orders of Uthman. They took the Quran of Abu Bakr as criterion and compared the other versions with it. Saeed ibn Aas dictated it, as his pronunciation resembled that of the Messenger of Allah (ṣ). Zaid wrote down the words according to the pronunciation of Saeed.

After a period of time, they realized that they needed the help of others as well so they invited eight other companions and together they became twelve persons.[2]

Ubayy ibn Kaab was one of the invitees and sometimes he dictated the verses for others. His Quran was also relied upon when it was in conformity. In doubtful instances, other companions were also referred to and their view was accepted only if two just males testified to its correctness.

---

[1] *Jamiul Usul*, Vol. 2, Pg. 504

[2] Suyuti, *Al-Itqan*, Vol. 1, Pg. 79

In some instances, they also relied on the views of Imam Ali (a).[1] Uthman supervised this process personally.

In this way a job of deep research was carried out as a result of which a Quran was compiled in a correct version. After that it was read out a number of times and compared with other copies and in the end a correct and accurate copy was finalized. It was then taken to be a standard to check and correct other copies.

After that Uthman ordered that it should be multiplied and a copy be sent to each Islamic metro. Thus they dispatched a copy of this Quran to all big cities and confiscated the ones extant over there and destroyed them.

In this way was realized the divine promise when God said:

إِنَّا نَحْنُ نَزَّلْنَا ٱلذِّكْرَ وَإِنَّا لَهُۥ لَحَٰفِظُونَ ۝

"Surely We have revealed the Reminder and We will most surely be its guardian." (15:9)

And also:

لَّا يَأْتِيهِ ٱلْبَٰطِلُ مِنۢ بَيْنِ يَدَيْهِ وَلَا مِنْ خَلْفِهِۦ ۖ تَنزِيلٌ مِّنْ حَكِيمٍ حَمِيدٍ ۝

"Falsehood shall not come to it from before it nor from behind it; a revelation from the Wise, the Praised One." (41:42)

And a collection of chapters and verses of Quran, without any alteration or additions or deletions, remained forever at the disposal of Muslims.

---

[1] Suyuti, *Al-Itqan*, Vol. 1, Pg. 79

DIMENSIONS OF MANNER AND MORALS OF THE HOLY PROPHET

The Prophet of Islam, from the aspect of ethics was the most eminent of men and a perfect human being. He possessed all good qualities to perfection and was pure of all evils and bad manners. The criteria of morals, which are mentioned in Islam and Quran, were personified in the being of His Eminence as Ayesha, his wife and other companions have also admitted.

Abu Darda says: I asked Ayesha about the morals and manners of the Holy Prophet (ṣ). She said: The morals of the Prophet were based on Quran. He was pleased with whatever Almighty Allah was pleased with and was angry at whatever Almighty Allah was angry with.[1]

He was having such excellent morals that Quran has praised him and said with regard to him:

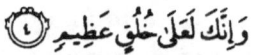

"And most surely you conform (yourself) to sublime morality." (68:4)

Although in this short treatise it is not possible to explain all the great manners and morals of the Messenger of Allah (ṣ), we would try to mention some of them here:

---

[1] *Al-Bidaya wan Nihaya*, Vol. 6, Pg. 37

Amirul Momineen (a) in the description of the Holy Prophet (s) says:

> *In generosity, he was ahead of all the people. He was the bravest of all. He was most truthful, loyal and had a kind disposition. He was the most social person. Whoever encountered him initially was influenced by his awe and after meeting him and being in his company used become fond of him. I have neither seen anyone like His Eminence before or after that.*[1]

Anas ibn Malik has said with regard to His Eminence: He had the most excellent manners, was most forbearing and generous of the people. It never happened that they asked something from him and he refused.[2]

Ayesha says: The Holy Prophet (s) was not bad mannered lacking morals and he was not of those who raised a hue and cry in the markets. He did not recompense a bad deed with a bad turn; on the contrary he always forgave mistakes.[3]

Husain ibn Ali (a) has narrated from his father that he said:

> *The Holy Prophet (s) was always cheerful, good natured and soft spoken; he was never nasty, bad natured and fault-picker and he ignored that which he did not like. He never disappointed anyone. He had purified his self from three things: Argumentation, extravagance and vain acts. In three things he had nothing to do with anyone: He was never harsh and a*

---

[1] *Biharul Anwar*, Vol. 16, Pg. 263

[2] *Uyunul Athar*, Vol. 2, Pg. 329

[3] *Uyunul Athar*, Vol. 2, Pg. 331

fault finder; he was never inclined to expose the secrets and hidden deficiencies of others; he never spoke, except when it entailed gaining heavenly rewards.[1]

Anas ibn Malik says: I went to the Holy Prophet (ṣ) to find him wearing a dress with a coarse edge. A Bedouin came to His Eminence, held his garment and pulled it roughly in such a way that I saw its signs on his shoulder; then he said: Muhammad, give me some of Allah's wealth. The Holy Prophet (ṣ) looked at him and smiled; then he ordered his men to give something to that man.[2]

Behavior with others

The Prophet of Islam (ṣ) diligently observed the manners of society. He was extremely humble and kind. He treated all Muslims equally, respected all and expressed his love for them. He asked the well being of those who were absent and visited the sick. He was present in funeral ceremonies. He accorded respect to children and greeted them first.

Abu Qatada has said with regard to His Eminence. Despite that grade and status, his humility exceeded that of other people. When he came to a group of companions, they stood up to pay respect to him, but he said: Do not honor me like the Persians who stand to pay respect to each other. I am the servant of God and I eat and drink like them. The Holy Prophet (ṣ) sometimes used to be astride a donkey and also made another person

---

[1] *Makarimul Akhlaq*, Vol. 1, Pg. 13
[2] *Al-Bidaya wan Nihaya*, Vol. 6, Pg. 43

sit behind him. He visited the poor to show his support and interacted with the underprivileged and even accepted invitations of slaves. When he entered an assembly, he took a seat in the last row.[1]

Jarir says with regard to the Messenger of Allah (s): He joked and spoke jovially with his friends. He also played with children and seated them in his lap. He accepted the invitation of all; visited the sick in the farthest corner of the city; accepted the excuse of those who committed mistakes.[2]

Anas says: The Holy Prophet (s) never stretched his legs before others. He saluted first whenever he met someone. He shook hands with his friends. He never stretched his legs before his companions. He accorded respect to all who came to meet him. Sometimes he used to spread out his cloak for the visitor to sit on or gave him that on which he was himself sitting. He addressed his companions with their agnomen (*Kunyah*) and called them with the best of names. He never interrupted when others spoke.[3]

Ibn Masud says: A person wanted to speak to the Holy Prophet (s), but began to tremble at the awe of His Eminence. The Prophet said: Take it easy. I am not a king. Rather, I am the son of a lady who ate dried meat.[4]

Abu Zar says: The Messenger of Allah (s) was seated among the companions when a poor man entered the

---

[1] *Uyunul Athar*, Vol. 2, Pg. 333

[2] *Uyunul Athar*, Vol. 2, Pg. 331

[3] *Uyunul Athar*, Vol. 2, Pg. 333

[4] *Biharul Anwar*, Vol. 16, Pg. 329

assembly; but he could not recognize the Holy Prophet (ṣ) without asking who the Prophet was.¹

Anas says: The Messenger of Allah (ṣ) passed by some children and greeted them.

He also says: When the Holy Prophet (ṣ) did not see one of the companions for three days, he inquired about his well being. If he were on a journey, he used to pray for him and if he was in town he used to go and meet him; if he was sick he paid a visit to him.²

Ayesha says: The Holy Prophet (ṣ) never beat up his servants and he never hit anyone except in Holy war (Jihad).³

Imam Ja'far Sadiq (a) said: The Messenger of Allah (ṣ) distributed his attention equally to all his companions and looked at them for equal duration of time.⁴

As a result of the good morals and manners of the Holy Prophet (ṣ) people were attracted to him and accepted his call as the Quran has said:

$$\text{فَبِمَا رَحْمَةٍ مِنَ اللَّهِ لِنتَ لَهُمْ وَلَوْ كُنتَ فَظًّا غَلِيظَ الْقَلْبِ لَانفَضُّوا مِنْ حَوْلِكَ فَاعْفُ عَنْهُمْ وَاسْتَغْفِرْ لَهُمْ وَشَاوِرْهُمْ فِي الْأَمْرِ فَإِذَا عَزَمْتَ فَتَوَكَّلْ عَلَى اللَّهِ إِنَّ اللَّهَ يُحِبُّ الْمُتَوَكِّلِينَ ﴿١٥٩﴾}$$

"Thus it is due to mercy from Allah that you deal with them gently, and had you been rough, hard hearted,

---

[1] *Biharul Anwar*, Vol. 16, Pg. 229

[2] *Makarimul Akhlaq*, Vol. 1, Pg. 19

[3] *Tabaqat Ibne Saad*, Vol. 1, Pg. 367

[4] *Biharul Anwar*, Vol. 16, Pg. 28

they would certainly have dispersed from around you; pardon them therefore and ask pardon for them, and take counsel with them in the affair; so when you have decided, then place your trust in Allah; surely Allah loves those who trust." (3:159)

Behavior of the Prophet with his family members

The treatment of Messenger of Allah (ṣ) at home to his wives and children was extremely kind and friendly. He expressed love to them, was always cheerful and good natured to them. He helped them in household chores. He was never harsh and overlooked their mistakes. He was very kind to children and even played with them.

Anas says: The Messenger of Allah (ṣ) helped the people his family members in household chores. He milked the goats, mended his shoes and did not transfer the burden of his tasks on others. He fed the animals, swept the house, tied the camels, ate with his servants, kneaded the dough and purchased groceries.[1]

Anas, the servant of the Messenger of Allah (ṣ) says: I was in the service of the Holy Prophet (ṣ) during his journey as well as at home. He never said: Why you did this? Or why you did not do that?[2]

Umrah says: I asked Ayesha: How did the Holy Prophet (ṣ) behave with his family members? She replied: He was most soft spoken and the most magnanimous person, he was cheerful and smiling.[3]

---

[1] *Uyunul Athar*, Vol. 2, Pg. 334

[2] *Al-Bidaya wan Nihaya*, Vol. 6, Pg. 39

[3] *Al-Bidaya wan Nihaya*, Vol. 6, Pg. 39

Jabir says: One day I came to the Holy Prophet (ṣ) and saw that Hasan and Husain were mounted on his back and he was moving on all fours and saying: You have the best of the mounts and you also are the best of the riders.[1]

Simplicity

The life of His Eminence was extremely simple and without any frills. His house was small and made up of clay. The floor was covered with a piece of mat and his food mostly consisted of barley bread and dates. Many a times it so happened that he did not even have this meager food and went hungry for a day or more. His clothes were simple and he mended his own shoes. But his simplicity was not due to poverty or deprivation, because he also possessed the strength to work and also had a share in war booty and public treasury. His simplicity was because he wanted to be at the same level as that of the people of the early period of Islam who were mostly poor. The Holy Prophet (ṣ) was the leader of Islamic community; therefore he refrained from luxuries so that it would be easy for others to bear difficulties. He distributed equitably the funds from public treasury. His and his relatives' share was never more than the share of others. On the contrary, sometimes he even gave his own share to the needy.

Ibn Abbas narrates:

One day Umar came to the Holy Prophet (ṣ) to find that the mat on which he was sitting had left an imprint on his side. He said: O Messenger of Allah (ṣ), if you had only

---

[1] *Biharul Anwar*, Vol. 43, Pg. 285

procured a nice carpet for yourself. The Holy Prophet (ṣ) replied: What do I have to do with the material world? My simile in the world is like the simile of a rider traveling on a hot day and who sits under a shade for an hour; then moves on.[1]

Ayesha says:

Sometimes a month passed on Aal Muhammad without their kitchen fires being kindled. Their food was nothing more than dates and water, except when cooked meat was brought for them.[2]

Ibn Abbas says: Sometimes many day and nights passed on the Prophet and his family when they did not have any food and they went to sleep hungry.[3]

Ayesha says: The Holy Prophet (ṣ) passed away when his family had been hungry continuously since the last three days had not eaten wheat bread.[4]

It is mentioned in *Uyunul Athar* that: The Messenger of Allah (ṣ) passed away from the world while his coat of mail was pawned with a Jew for a dirham to cover his household expenses.[5]

Worship

The Messenger of Allah (ṣ) was the most devoted person to worship and he accorded great importance to the worship of Allah. He was very fond of ritual prayer and

---

[1] *Makarimul Akhlaq*, Vol. 1, Pg. 25

[2] *Al-Bidaya wan Nihaya*, Vol. 6, Pg. 58

[3] *Uyunul Athar*, Vol. 2, Pg. 335

[4] *Al-Bidaya wan Nihaya*, Vol. 6, Pg. 57

[5] *Uyunul Athar*, Vol. 2, Pg. 334

he remarked: The light of my eyes is in ritual prayer.¹

He performed the obligatory prayers at the earliest hour and with concentration. He also recited the supererogatory and recommended prayers. He used to rise up in the last part of the night as Almighty Allah says in Quran:

$$\text{وَمِنَ ٱلَّيْلِ فَتَهَجَّدْ بِهِ نَافِلَةً لَّكَ عَسَىٰٓ أَن يَبْعَثَكَ رَبُّكَ مَقَامًا مَّحْمُودًا ۝}$$

"And during a part of the night, pray Tahajjud (the midnight prayer) beyond what is incumbent on you; maybe your Lord will raise you to a position of great glory." (17:79)

The Holy Prophet (ṣ) was always engrossed in the remembrance of God. During the blessed month of Ramadan he paid more attention to ritual prayer and worship of God. He prayed so much that his legs got swollen and finally the following verse was revealed:

$$\text{طه ۝ مَآ أَنزَلْنَا عَلَيْكَ ٱلْقُرْءَانَ لِتَشْقَىٰٓ ۝}$$

"Ta Ha. We have not revealed the Quran to you that you may be unsuccessful." (20:1-2)

Mughira ibn Shoba says with regard to the worship of the Prophet:

He stood in ritual prayer at such length that his legs were swollen and he was told: Has God not forgiven your past and future sins? He replied: Should I not be a thankful servant of Allah?²

---

¹ *Jamiul Ahadith Shia*, Vol. 20, Pg. 25
² *Al-Bidaya wan Nihaya*, Vol. 6, Pg. 60

Anas says: The Messenger of Allah (ṣ) used to always be engrossed in the remembrance of God and he never committed any vain act.[1]

Imam Ja'far Sadiq (a) says:

> The Messenger of Allah (ṣ) was in the chamber of Ummu Salma one night. Ummu Salma awoke and could not find the Holy Prophet (ṣ) in bed. She became suspicious and arose and searched for him around the house. She found him in a corner; he was standing with his hands raised to the heavens; he was weeping and saying: O Allah, never take away from me the good sense of doing good.[2]

He also said:

> It was the habit of the Holy Prophet (ṣ) that he used to remain in Etekaf at the Masjid during the last ten days of the month of Ramadan. A tent was pitched therein from him. He used to gather his bed and get ready for worship.[3]

Abu Bakr said to the Prophet:

O Messenger of Allah (ṣ), your hair has grayed. He replied: Surah Hud, Surah Waqiyah, Surah Mursalat, Surah Naba and Surah Takwir have caused it.[4]

Abu Zar says:

The Messenger of Allah (ṣ) stood in prayer throughout the night and recited the following verse: *"If Thou*

---

[1] *Al-Bidaya wan Nihaya*, Vol. 6, Pg. 46
[2] *Biharul Anwar*, Vol. 6, Pg. 217
[3] *Biharul Anwar*, Vol. 6, Pg. 273
[4] *Al-Bidaya wan Nihaya*, Vol. 6, Pg. 67

shouldst chastise them, then surely they are Thy servants; and if Thou shouldst forgive them, then surely Thou art the Mighty, the Wise."[1]

Morals and manners of the Prophet in Quran

The Holy Prophet (ṣ) always entreated to Almighty Allah with humility and sincerity to bestow him with good manners. In his supplications, His Eminence said: My Lord, improve my manners and morals. He also prayed: O Lord, Keep me free of bad morals and manners.

God answered his prayers and revealed the Quran on him and disciplined him through Quran and the Quran became his nature. Saad ibn Hisham says: I asked Ayesha about the morals and manners of the Holy Prophet (ṣ). She said: Have you not read the Quran? I asked: Why? She said: The morals of the Prophet are same as Quran.

Morals of the Prophet are taken directly from revelation and Quran. By way of examples see the following:

خُذِ ٱلْعَفْوَ وَأْمُرْ بِٱلْعُرْفِ وَأَعْرِضْ عَنِ ٱلْجَٰهِلِينَ ۝

"Take to forgiveness and enjoin good and turn aside from the ignorant." (7:199)

إِنَّ ٱللَّهَ يَأْمُرُ بِٱلْعَدْلِ وَٱلْإِحْسَٰنِ

"Surely Allah enjoins the doing of justice and the doing of good (to others)..." (16:90)

وَٱصْبِرْ وَمَا صَبْرُكَ إِلَّا بِٱللَّهِ

"And be patient and your patience is not but by (the assistance of) Allah." (16:127)

---

[1] *Al-Bidaya wan Nihaya*, Vol. 6, Pg. 65

$$\text{وَٱصْبِرْ عَلَىٰ مَآ أَصَابَكَۖ إِنَّ ذَٰلِكَ مِنْ عَزْمِ ٱلْأُمُورِ ۝}$$

"...and bear patiently that which befalls you; surely these acts require courage." (31:17)

$$\text{وَلَمَن صَبَرَ وَغَفَرَ إِنَّ ذَٰلِكَ لَمِنْ عَزْمِ ٱلْأُمُورِ ۝}$$

"And whoever is patient and forgiving, these most surely are actions due to courage." (42:43)

$$\text{فَٱعْفُ عَنْهُمْ وَٱصْفَحْۚ إِنَّ ٱللَّهَ يُحِبُّ ٱلْمُحْسِنِينَ ۝}$$

"...so pardon them and turn away; surely Allah loves those who do good (to others)." (5:13)

$$\text{وَلْيَعْفُوا۟ وَلْيَصْفَحُوٓا۟ۗ أَلَا تُحِبُّونَ أَن يَغْفِرَ ٱللَّهُ لَكُمْ}$$

"...and they should pardon and turn away. Do you not love that Allah should forgive you?" (24:22)

$$\text{ٱدْفَعْ بِٱلَّتِى هِىَ أَحْسَنُ فَإِذَا ٱلَّذِى بَيْنَكَ وَبَيْنَهُۥ عَدَٰوَةٌ كَأَنَّهُۥ وَلِىٌّ حَمِيمٌ}$$

"Repel (evil) with what is best, when lo! he between whom and you was enmity would be as if he were a warm friend." (41:34)

$$\text{وَٱلْكَٰظِمِينَ ٱلْغَيْظَ وَٱلْعَافِينَ عَنِ ٱلنَّاسِ}$$

"...and those who restrain (their) anger and pardon men." (3:134)

$$\text{ٱجْتَنِبُوا۟ كَثِيرًا مِّنَ ٱلظَّنِّ إِنَّ بَعْضَ ٱلظَّنِّ إِثْمٌۖ وَلَا تَجَسَّسُوا۟ وَلَا يَغْتَب بَّعْضُكُم بَعْضًا}$$

"...avoid most of suspicion, for surely suspicion in some cases is a sin, and do not spy nor let some of you backbite others." (49:12)

In the above verses and hundreds of other verses Almighty Allah has mentioned good morals and manners and advised the Prophet and his followers to follow them and He has also listed the bad habits and morals and asked them to keep away from them. The Holy Prophet (ṣ) himself observed good manners and morals and kept away from bad manners and morals, in such a way that he can be called as the personification of the morals and manners of Quran as Ayesha had described him with this title. That is why Almighty Allah said with regard to him:

$$وَإِنَّكَ لَعَلَىٰ خُلُقٍ عَظِيمٍ$$

"And most surely you conform (yourself) to sublime morality." (68:4)

The Holy Prophet (ṣ) himself acted on good manners and by his word and speech, continuously advised the Muslims to observe good manners and morals and said: I have been sent to perfect morals. Therefore hundreds of traditions have been recorded from the Prophet of Islam with regard to ethical problems and recorded in books of traditions.

Good morals and preferable manners can be considered as most important factors of his popularity and influence among the Muslims. Since they did what he told them to do and agreed to what he said. The same point is mentioned in Quran:

$$فَبِمَا رَحْمَةٍ مِنَ اللَّهِ لِنْتَ لَهُمْ وَلَوْ كُنْتَ فَظًّا غَلِيظَ الْقَلْبِ لَانْفَضُّوا مِنْ حَوْلِكَ$$

"Thus it is due to mercy from Allah that you deal with them gently, and had you been rough, hard hearted, they would certainly have dispersed from around you..." (3:159)

Some Qualities of the Prophet

Faiz Kashani has narrated from Abul Bakhtari that he said with regard to the Prophet: The Prophet never spoke ill of the believers and if by chance he uttered something harsh, he made amends for it immediately by doing a good turn to them. He never cursed his women or servants. During battles, His Eminence was urged to curse the enemies, but he said: I have been sent for mercy and guidance and not to curse. Whenever he was suggested to curse Muslims or infidels, especially or generally he used to rather pray for them.

He never beat anyone; except that it should be for the sake of God. He never sought revenge to any offence, except if it had been an affront to God. He never had two options to choose from, but that he chose the easiest of them. Except that it should be a cause of sin or breaking off of relations as he kept away from it more than anyone else. No free man or slave ever came to him with a request, but that he hastened to help him or her immediately.

Anas says: By God, the Messenger of Allah (s) never ordered me to do something which I did not like. And he never said: Why didn't you do it? And if his family members scolded me for that job, he said: Leave him, because there is a job he has accomplished. The Messenger of Allah (s) never spoke in a harsh manner, if the bed was made for him, he slept on it and if not, he slept on bare floor.

His manners were such that he greeted all those he met. He never interrupted others while they spoke and waited patiently for others to finish speaking.

When he shook hands he never retrieved his hand before the other person. When he met any of the companions, he shook hands with them. He took their hand in his hands and interlaced his fingers with theirs and held them firm. He never arose or sat down without mentioning God. If a person came to meet him when he was praying, he shortened his prayer and asked: Do you want something from me? After fulfilling his need, he again continued his prayer. He never occupied a special place in assemblies and he took any seat that was vacant. He never stretched his legs in front of others, lest there should be less space for others; except when ample space was available. He mostly sat facing the Qibla. He greeted all those who came to meet him and he even spread out his cloak for the visitor to sit on even though he was not related to him. Whoever came to meet him was urged to sit in the seat of the Prophet. He was respectful to one and all in such a way that each of them was convinced that he or she was the most respected person in view of the Prophet. He paid equal attention to all those who were present in the assembly. His gathering was in a halo of modesty, humility and trust. Allah has said with regard to him:

"Thus it is due to mercy from Allah that you deal with them gently, and had you been rough, hard hearted, they would certainly have dispersed from around you."

He addressed his companions with their agnomen (*Kunniyat*) in order to accord them respect and please them. He selected an agnomen for whosoever who did not have it already. He even selected agnomens for ladies who had children and those who did not have any children. He gave agnomen even to children in order to please them. He was angered by people only after a long time and used to become happy very soon. He was most beneficial for the people. He never raised his voice in his assemblies. When he arose from a gathering, he said: "Glory be to You, O Allah, and praise be to You. I witness that there is no god except You. I seek Your forgiveness and turn to You in repentance." He then said: Jibraeel has taught me as such.[1]

Forgiveness despite having the power of revenge

The Holy Prophet (s) was the most forbearing person. He was most inclined than others to forgive despite having the power to retaliate. One day he distributed gold and silver necklaces among his companions, which were a part of public treasury. A Bedouin stood up and objected: Has God not ordered you to observe justice? I do not consider you just in this distribution. He said: Who else other than me would deal with you in such a just manner? When that man wanted to go away, the Prophet said: Call him back. Jabir has narrated that the Holy Prophet (s), after the Battle of Hunain distributed silver coins among the people, which were obtained as war booty. A man said: O Messenger of Allah (s), distribute equitably. The Holy Prophet (s) said: If I am not just, who else would be? If it is so, I would be causing harm. At this moment Umar stood up and said: O Messenger of Allah (s), he is a hypocrite; allow me to strike off his head. The Holy Prophet (s) disallowed him and said: I seek the refuge of Allah from committing such a deed as people would say: Muhammad kills his own companions.

---

[1] Mulla Mohsin Faiz Kashani, *Muhajjatul Baidha fee Tahdheebul Ahyaa*, Vol. 4, Pg. 128-132

During one of the battles, when the Messenger of Allah (s) was in a safe place away from the battle, an opponent came and stood at his head with a naked sword and said: Who can save you from me? The Holy Prophet (s) just said: God. At that moment the sword fell from his hand. The Prophet picked it up immediately and said: Now who can save you from me? He replied: Although the sword is in your hand, you are the best wielder of the sword.

He said: Say: I testify that there is no god, except Allah. He said: I will not fight you and I am going out of the battlefield. The Holy Prophet (s) left him alone. That man went back to his people and said: I am coming from the best of men.

Anas says: A Jew woman decided to poison the Holy Prophet (s) through poisoned roasted meat and she came to His Eminence with this intent. The Holy Prophet (s) asked about her intention. She said: I want to eliminate you. He said: God forbid that such thing should really happen. Companions asked: Did you not eliminate her? He replied: No.

His Eminence, Ali (a) said: The Messenger of Allah (s) told me, Zubair and Miqdad to reach Raudha Khak as soon as possible. There we would see a litter with a woman carrying a letter. We should take the letter from her and bring it to the Prophet. We set out immediately and reached the stated place soon. We decried the litter on which that woman was seated. We brought her down and said: Give us the letter that you are carrying. She said: I have nothing with me. We said: You are definitely carrying a letter; give it to us or we would kill or strip you and take it from you. She was compelled to take out the letter she had concealed in her hair and hand it over to us. We brought the letter to the Holy Prophet (s). He opened it and it was written therein: This is the letter of Hatib ibn Abi Balta to some polytheists of Mecca. The letter divulged to the polytheists an administrative secret of Muslims. The Messenger of Allah (s) got Hatib arrested and asked: Why have you written this letter? He replied: O Messenger of Allah (s), emigrants who have migrated from Mecca to Medina, have relatives in Mecca who can defend their family members there. But I don't have any supporters in Mecca. Through this letter, I intended to do a good turn to the Meccans so they might have a soft corner for my family in Mecca. What I did was not due to infidelity or apostasy. The Holy Prophet (s) accepted his excuse and said: You are right. Umar ibn Khattab, who was present there, said: Allow me to execute this hypocrite. The Holy Prophet (s) said: This man had participated in Battle of Badr; it is possible that he may gain divine forgiveness.

The Holy Prophet (s) said:

> *Do not narrate any defects of my companions to me, because I would like to meet you with a pure heart.*[1]

Moderation and pardon

A Bedouin came to the Holy Prophet (s) and asked for something. The Holy Prophet (s) gave something and asked: Have I done a favor to you? He replied: No, you have not. Muslims became furious at the audacity of that man and wanted to punish him. The Holy Prophet (s)

---

[1] *Muhajjatul Baidha*, Vol. 4, Pg. 145-148

signaled that no one should do anything to him. After that he arose and entered his chamber and sent someone to bring that man. Then he gave another quantity to him and then asked: Have I done a favor to you, are you happy? He replied: Yes, O Messenger of Allah (ṣ), you have done a favor to me; may God give you a good reward for it. The Holy Prophet (ṣ) said: You uttered those words and angered the companions; I feel that it would be appropriate if you should repeat these words to them so that they may not harbor malice to you. That man said: I will do that.

The next day that man came to the Masjid. The Holy Prophet (ṣ) told the companions: Yesterday you heard those words from this gentleman; I invited him home and gave him some more till he was satisfied. The Bedouin also said: Yes, I am satisfied; may God give you a good reward.

The Messenger of Allah (ṣ) said: The simile of myself and this man is the like the simile of a man whose camel has fled. People chase the camel to apprehend it, but as much they chase it, as much further it flees. The camel owner tells the people: Leave my camel alone. I know better how to control it. At that moment he takes up a bunch of grass and waves it at the camel and in this way calms down the beast gradually. The camel slowly kneels down before him. Then he puts the litter on its back and mounts it. I also dealt with that Bedouin in the same manner. If you had killed him on hearing those words, you would have entered Hell.[1]

---

[1] *Muhajjatul Baidha*, Vol. 4, Pg. 149

Generosity and forgiveness

When Imam Ali (a) described the fine qualities of the Holy Prophet (s); he said as follows: He was the most forgiving and generous of all. He was most cheerful, truthful, loyal, soft-natured and magnanimous. His awe left its mark on the people. Anyone who came across him started liking him. He had no equal before or after him. He did not spurn any beggar without giving him anything. A person asked something from His Eminence, and he was given a large number of sheep. That man returned to his folks and remarked: Accept the faith that Muhammad is propagating. He is generous in giving and he does not fear poverty.

He never said 'no' to anyone who asked him for something. One day seventy thousand dirhams were presented to him and he distributed all of it the same day. A beggar asked for something but since he had nothing, he told him: Presently you may buy whatever you need on credit, and as soon I get something, I would repay your debt. Umar said: O Messenger of Allah (s), God has not asked for anything on which you have no control. The Prophet was not pleased by this suggestion. The beggar said: O Messenger of Allah (s), be generous and do not fear poverty. The Holy Prophet (s) smiled at these words and the signs of joy became apparent on his face.

When Battle of Hunain was over, Bedouins of the surrounding area gathered around the Prophet and asked for a share in the booty. The Holy Prophet (s) was forced to take refuge in a tree and they even snatched his cloak. He said: Give back my cloak. If I had as many camels as these stones I would distribute them among you and you will not find me miserly, lying and timid.[1]

---

[1] *Muhajjatul Baidha*, Vol. 4, Pg. 149-150

Imam Ja'far Sadiq (a) said: A man came to the Holy Prophet (s) and gave twelve dirhams. Since his garments had become old, he gave the twelve dirhams to Ali Ibn Abi Talib (a) and said: Buy a dress for me. Ali (a) says: I went to the market and purchased a dress for twelve dirhams and returned to the Prophet. He looked at the dress and said: I don't like it. Would the seller take it back? I said: I don't know. Then I took the dress back and said: The Messenger of Allah (s) did not like this dress, can you cancel the transaction? He replied: Yes. He took the dress and returned the twelve dirhams. I took the money and returned them to the Holy Prophet (s). Then I came to the market with him to buy another dress. On the way we saw a female slave weeping by the roadside. The Holy Prophet (s) asked what the mater was and she said: My master had given four dirhams to me and asked me to make some purchases. But somehow I lost the money. Now I cannot dare to go back home. The Messenger of Allah (s) gave her four dirhams and said: Go home.

After that we continued on our way to the market and bought a dress from His Eminence, for four dirhams. The Prophet put on the dress and said: Praise be to Allah. On way back home we saw a man having nothing to wear and he was saying: God will dress in garment of Paradise one who gives me something to wear. The Messenger of Allah (s) gave the dress he had purchased for himself.

We went to the market for the second time and bought a dress from the remaining four dirhams. He put it on and thanked the Almighty. We were returning home when we saw that same slave girl and she still sitting there. The Messenger of Allah (s) asked: Why have you not returned home? She replied: Since I was very late I feared beating. The Holy Prophet (ṣ) said: Come I will accompany you home and recommend your case with your master. He came to the house of that slave girl and said: Peace be on you O people of the house. No one replied till he repeated it thrice. The third time, the owner of the house responded: And peace be on you, O Messenger of Allah (ṣ). The Prophet asked: Why did you not reply the first time? He replied: I heard your Salam but I wanted you to repeat it. The Messenger of Allah (ṣ) said: Your slave girl has returned late; do not punish her for it. He said: I have emancipated this slave girl as a mark of respect for you. The Messenger of Allah (ṣ) said: Praise be to Allah. I have not seen any twelve dirhams more blessed than these. Two persons got clothes and a slave girl was freed.[1]

Imam Muhammad Baqir (a) said: A beggar approached the Messenger of Allah (ṣ) and asked for something. Since the Holy Prophet (ṣ) was not having anything to fulfill the needs of that beggar, he told the companions: Is there anyone who would lend me something? A person said: O Messenger of Allah (ṣ), I will. He said: Give four loads of dates to this beggar; I will return them to you later on. The Ansari man handed over the dates to the beggar. After some days, he came to the Prophet and demanded him to return the dates that he had loaned. The Messenger of Allah (ṣ) said: I will do so if God wills. The Ansari man approached him a number of times asking for his dates and the Prophet every time assured: I will do so if God wills. After a period of time he again

---

[1] *Biharul Anwar*, Vol. 16, Pg. 14

came to the Prophet and asked: Why do you not fulfill my demand? The Prophet said: I will do so if God wills. Ansari man said: Till when would you go on saying if God wills, if God wills? The Prophet smiled and told the companions: Is there anyone who can lend me a quantity of dates? A man agreed and the Prophet told him to give eight loads of dates to that man. That Ansari said: I am not asking for additional loads. He said: They also belong to you.

Modesty

In spite of having such a great position, the Messenger of Allah (ṣ) was an extremely humble person. Ibn Aamir says: I saw the Messenger of Allah (ṣ) during the stoning of Satans (*Jamarat*). He was astride a camel and was stoning without exercising any sort of formalities.

He rode a donkey without a saddle and at the same time had another person with him. He visited the sick and attended funerals; he accepted the invitation of slaves; mended his own shoes and patched his clothes. He cooperated with his family members in household chores. Companions did not stand up to pay respect to him as they knew that he did not like it. He greeted children. Sometimes when a person trembled in his awe, he said: Take it easy, I am not a king. I am the son of a lady who ate dried meat. He sat among companions in such a way as if he was one of them. A poor man entered the assembly; but could not recognize the Prophet so that he may ask him about something. Hence companions fixed a special place for him.

Ayesha said to the Prophet: While eating, recline on something so that you are comfortable. The Messenger of

Allah (s) brought his head near the ground and said: No, I eat and sit like slaves.

He accepted the invitation of all those who invited him for dinner. When he sat with companions, if they talked about matters related to the hereafter, he spoke with them but if they discussed food and drinks or worldly matters, he joined their discussion as a friendly gesture.[1]

Imam Ja'far Sadiq (a) said: Once a foster sister of the Holy Prophet (s) came to him. He became very happy to see her, spread out his sheet for her and made her sit thereon and talked happily with her. When she left, her brother arrived. The Holy Prophet (s) did not display as much welcome for him. When companions asked he said: "She is more respectful to her father."[2]

Prophet's activities inside the house

Imam Husain (a) says: I asked my father about the jobs the Prophet did inside his house. He said: How he spent his time at home was left to his own discretion. When he entered the house, he divided his time into three parts: a part for worship; a part for his family and remaining for his personal chores.

From the time reserved for himself also, he divided it between himself and others and he fulfilled their needs. In the part reserved from others, he gave first preference to the excellent and religious persons and in that also he gave precedence to each of them as per his merit. Some of them had one need and some two and others had more. He fulfilled their demands and solved their problems and

---

[1] *Muhajjatul Baidha*, Vol. 4, Pg. 151-152

[2] *Biharul Anwar*, Vol. 16, Pg. 281

problems related to people in general. He decided a matter and then said: Those who are present must convey the mentioned problems to those who are absent. He also said: Convey to me the needs of those who have no access to me. One who conveys the needs of the needy to the ruler; Almighty Allah on Judgment Day makes his feet more steadfast. In this manner, problems were presented to him and he did not allow that during this time they should discuss other matters. In these meetings, companions used to be present as visitors, but they did not disperse without getting social and intellectual benefits.[1]

Prophet's activities outside the house

Imam Hasan (a) said: At that moment I asked my father what the Prophet did outside the house? He replied: The Messenger of Allah (ṣ) never spoke, except when it was beneficial. He was such that companions became attached to him and did not disperse from him. He accorded respect to the leader of every tribe and retained him as the head of his clan. He warned people about discord and mischief. He used to protect himself from people without misbehaving with them. He used to be affable to his companions. He used to be informed about news and happenings in the society through public. He supported good works and condemned the evil acts and deeds.

He used to exercise caution in all matters and was never careless, lest those who are actually in charge of them should be careless and lazy and he was prepared in all circumstances. He was never shortcoming in truth and

---

[1] *Makarimul Akhlaq*, Vol. 1, Pg. 11

neither did he exceed the limits. His relatives were the best of human beings. The most honorable among them were those who dispensed good advice and were well wishers. The best in his view was one who was most helpful to his brothers.[1]

Behavior of the Prophet in gatherings

Imam Hasan (a) said: Then I asked my father about the behavior of the Prophet in gatherings. He replied: He never sat down or stood up except with the mention of God. He never reserved a special place for himself in a gathering and he prohibited such a thing. When he entered an assembly, he took any place that was vacant and advised the same to his companions. He paid equal attention to all those who were present there, so that no one should think that others are being preferred. He used to wait patiently for the other person to conclude his statement before he would speak up. Anyone who asked him for something either had his need fulfilled or he pleased him through his words. People used to be satisfied with his manners and he was like a father to them. All were in fact equal in his view. His gathering was full of forbearance, modesty, patience and trust. In his gathering, voices were not raised. The down-trodden people were not humiliated and their mistakes were overlooked. The people of the gathering were equal and as brothers and in observance of piety, they competed with each other. They observed absolute humility. They accorded respect to the elderly and were kind to youngsters. They preferred the needy over their own selves. They looked after outsiders who visited their town.[2]

---

[1] *Makarimul Akhlaq*, Vol. 1, Pg. 12
[2] *Makarimul Akhlaq*, Vol. 1, Pg. 12

Behavior of the Prophet towards people in a gathering

Now Imam Hasan (a) asked about the behavior of the Prophet with his neighbors. Imam Ali (a) said: He was always jolly in nature, cheerful and soft-natured. He was never harsh and cruel. He never shouted or spoke ill of anyone. He did not pick faults and was also not a flatterer.

He used to ignore what he disliked. He did not disappoint others and did not kill the hopes of the hopeful. He refrained from three things: Arguments, speaking too much and talking of useless things. In three things, he had nothing to do with anyone: He never condemned or scolded anyone nor picked fault in anyone. He never spoke except when it carried divine rewards. When he spoke, the people of the gathering used to become absolutely quiet as if a bird was sitting on their heads. When he became quiet people spoke up, but did not object or argue with him. When his lips moved, all fell silent so that he may conclude his statement. When the people laughed, the Messenger of Allah (s) also laughed and if they expressed astonishment he also expressed amazement. He tolerated the harsh words of some people and demands of strangers. Companions also, for the sake of Prophet and to attract his attention helped strangers and needy persons. The Messenger of Allah (s) used to advise the companions that they should do their best to fulfill the needs of the needy. He did not accept the adoration of anyone, except that it should be for a favor. He never interrupted anyone before he could conclude what he was saying.[1]

---

[1] *Makarimul Akhlaq*, Vol. 1, Pg. 13

Behavior of the Prophet with the youth

The Holy Prophet of Islam (ṣ) valued the young people and the power of youth and he time and again advised his companions to know the value of youth. That they should accord respect to their personalities and pay special attention to their upbringing, give them responsibilities and protect them. The Prophet also did the same, so that others would follow his example. We present some examples of this as follows:

In the early period of Islam, Asad ibn Zurarah and Zakwan came from Medina to Mecca. They met the Holy Prophet (ṣ) during one of the rituals and accepted Islam through his propagation and recited the formula of faith. When they decided to return to Medina, they requested the Holy Prophet (ṣ) to send someone with them to teach the people Quran and invite them to Islam. The Messenger of Allah (ṣ) appointed Musab ibn Umair, who although a youth was well versed with the Holy Quran, to accompany Asad and Zakwan to Medina and to propagate Islam. Also that he should lead the prayers and recite the Quran and sermons to them. Musab came to Medina and initiated his propagation. Since he was a worthy youth, energetic, accomplished and determined, people, especially the youth accepted his call and Islam became popular in Medina. After some days, Musab wrote to the Messenger of Allah (ṣ) about the conversion of the people of Medina to Islam.[1]

The Holy Prophet (ṣ) at the time of departing for the Battle of Hunain appointed Itab ibn Usaid, a youth of twenty-one, as the governor and congregation leader of

---

[1] *Biharul Anwar*, Vol. 19, Pg. 10-11

Mecca and asked him: Do you know, where and on whom have I appointed you as governor? I have appointed you as the ruler of the sanctuary of God; after that he repeated thrice: Be nice to the folks of the sanctuary.

He fixed for him a salary of a dirham per day. In the administration of Mecca, Itab was kind and merciful to believers and was strict and rough with the opponents. He was very strict about attendance in congregation prayer. He delivered very nice sermons. One day he said in his speech: The Prophet has fixed a dirham for me every day and I remain content with it without asking anyone for more.[1]

A few days before his passing away, the Messenger of Allah (ṣ) decided to dispatch an army to confront the Romans and with this aim gave the command of the huge army to Usamah ibn Zaid, a boy of seventeen. He was made the commander of all emigrants (*Muhajireen*) and helpers (*Ansar*). He told him: Camp at such and such place on the outskirts of the town till people join your forces and he ordered emigrants and helpers to join Usamah's army and not to keep away from it. Some companions did not join under the pretext that Usamah was too young to be a commander. When this information reached the Holy Prophet (ṣ), in spite of the fact that he was severely ill, he came to the Masjid, mounted the pulpit and after praise and glorification of God said:

What is it that I hear about the commandership of Usamah? And under the pretext that he is too young,

---
[1] *Seerat Halabi*, Vol. 3, Pg. 120

some are not joining his army. Previously also you had objected to the commandership of his father. By God, Usamah is indeed capable of leading the army and he is the best for it. Join his army and obey his commands.[1]

---

[1] *Biharul Anwar*, Vol. 21, Pg. 410; *Tarikh Yaqubi*, Vol. 2, Pg. 113

BIBLIOGRAPHY

1. Ibn Athir, *Al-Kamil Fit-Tarikh*, Daar Saadir, Beirut 1385 A.H.
2. Ibn Athir Jazari, Muhammad, *Jamiul Usul*, Second Edition: Darul Fikr, Beirut 1403 A.H.
3. Ibn Kathir, Abul Fida Ismail, *Siratun Nabawiyya*, Darul Mauqa, 1396 A.H.
4. Ibn Kathir, Abul Fida Ismail, *Al-Bidaya wan Nihaya*, Daar Ahya Thurathul Arabiyya, Beirut, 1408 A.H.
5. Ibn Saad, *At-tabaqaat al-Kubra*, Daar Saadir, Beirut 1380 A.H.
6. Ibn Shahr Ashob, Muhammad ibn Ali, *Manaqib Aale Abi Talib*, Second Edition, Intisharaat Zil Qurba, [Undated]
7. Ibn Hisham, *As-Seeratun Nabawiyyah*, Matba Mustafa Baati, Egypt, 1355 A.H.
8. Bulazari, Ahmad ibn Yahya, *Ansabul Ashraaf*, First Edition, Mausisa Aalami, Beirut, 1394 A.H.
9. Harati, Hasan ibn Ali ibn Husain, *Tohafful Uqul*, Kitab Faroshi Islamiya, Tehran 1384 A.H.
10. Hurre Amili, Muhammad ibn Hasan, *Wasailush Shia*, First Edition, Mausisa Aale Bayt, Qum, 1409 A.H.
11. Haqqi, Ismail, *Tafsir Ruhul Bayan*, Daar Ahya Thurathul Arabiyya, Beirut, [Undated]
12. Halabi, Ali ibn Burhanuddin, *As-Seerah Halabiyyah*, Matba Mustafa Muhammad, Egypt, [Undated]
13. Cambridge University, *History of Iran from Seljuqs to the downfall of Sasanid Empire*, Vol. 3, Muasisa Amir Kabir, Tehran [Undated]
14. Suyuti, Jalaluddin, *Al-Itqan fee Uloomil Quran*, Daarul Marifa, Beirut, [Undated]

15. Tabatabai, Allamah Sayyid Muhammad Husain, *Al-Mizan Fee Tafsiril Quran*, First Edition, Darul Kutubil Islamiyyah, Tehran. [Undated]

16. Subhi Salih, *Nahjul Balagha*, Darul Hujra, Qom, [Undated]

17. Tabarsi, Fazl ibn Hasan, *Makarimul Akhlaq*, Mausisa Aalami, Kerbala. [Undated]

18. Faiz Kashani, Mulla Mohsin, *Al-Muhajjatul Baidha fee Tahdhibul Ahya*, Second Edition, Intisharaat Islami, Qom, [Undated]

19. Qashiri Nishaburi, Muslim ibn Hajjaj, *Sahih Muslim*, Second Edition, Daar Ahya Thurathul Arabiyya, Beirut, [Undated]

20. Katani, Abdul Hayy, *At-Tarateebul Idariya*, Daar Ahya Thurathul Arabiyya, Beirut, [Undated]

21. Kulaini, Muhammad ibn Yaqub, *Al-Kafi*, Daarul Kutub Islamiyya, Tehran, 1388 A.H.

22. Majlisi, Allamah Muhammad Baqir, *Biharul Anwar*, Al-Maktabatul Islamiyya, Tehran, 1386 A.H.

23. Muizzi, Ismail, *Jamiul Ahadith Shia*, First Edition, Tehran, 1370 A.H.

24. Will Durant, *History of Civilization*, Second Edition, Intisharaat Aalami Farhangi, Tehran, 1368

25. Yaqubi, Ahmad ibn Yaqub, *Tarikh Yaqubi*, Daar Sadir, Beirut, 1379 A.H.

www.ingramcontent.com/pod-product-compliance
Lightning Source LLC
LaVergne TN
LVHW041935070526
838199LV00051BA/2797